Big Foot
and the
Bentley

M L SCHOLL

Copyright © 2022 Mary L Scholl

All rights reserved.

ISBN: 9798842474677

DEDICATION

Brad and Diane Hill. Brad's been telling stories all of his life, and Diane supports his every whim.
They are not only loyal members of my fan club, but Brad has consented to being Bernie on my covers, along with his Tucker.

ACKNOWLEDGMENT

My uncle, Brad Hill, for allowing me to use him as the face of Bernie in this, my newest, series…

Special thanks to the CITRUS COUNTY CRUISERS!
I showed up unannounced to one of their regular shows and was treated to good old Southern hospitality. I asked nosy questions about everything from insurance to the internal workings of their organization.
The President, CINDY BOTA, told me they have been meeting and showing for nearly 50 years!
Her only question for me, when I had finished relating the tale of Bernie, the Big Foot and the Bentley was
"Why a Bentley?"
After wandering through the sampling of their nearly 300 beautiful cars, I wandered through the internet – and fell in love – with an alliteratively appropriate baby-blue Bentley.
A story was born...

Table of Contents

CHAPTER 1	**SATURDAY**	9
CHAPTER 2	**SUNDAY**	13
CHAPTER 3	**MONDAY**	23
CHAPTER 4	**WEDNESDAY**	31
CHAPTER 5	**THURSDAY**	37
CHAPTER 6	**FRIDAY**	45
CHAPTER 7	**SATURDAY**	55
CHAPTER 8	**SUNDAY**	63
CHAPTER 9	**MONDAY**	69
CHAPTER 10	**TUESDAY**	75
CHAPTER 11	**WEDNESDAY**	77
CHAPTER 12	**THURSDAY**	84
CHAPTER 13	**FRIDAY**	91
CHAPTER 14	**SATURDAY**	99
CHAPTER 15	**WEDNESDAY**	107
CHAPTER 16	**THURSDAY**	113
CHAPTER 17	***STILL* THURSDAY**	125
CHAPTER 18	**FRIDAY**	135
CHAPTER 19	**SATURDAY**	139
CHAPTER 20	**MONDAY**	149

CHAPTER 21 TUESDAY 153

CHAPTER 22 WEDNESDAY 157

CHAPTER 23 THURSDAY 165

CHAPTER 24 STILL THURSDAY 173

CHAPTER 25 FRIDAY 181

CHARACTERS

Bernice – Bernie's Daughter

Bernie Murphy – Handsome Irishman returns

Carl – Tina's uncle

Catherine – Retired psychologist

Charlie – Deputy

Dan – Detective

Doris – Pete's wife

Gruagach – (grew-uh-gosh)

Harold and Caroleen – Car Club, owned Bentley

Michael – Tina's cousin

Myrna and Kevin – Car Club

Patty Decker– Grouchy old woman

Pete – Maintenance man at the park

Ralph - Bernie's brother

Roger – Bernie's son

Tina – Neighbor woman

Big Foot and the Bentley

BIG FOOT AND THE BENTLEY

CHAPTER 1   SATURDAY

Bernie Murphy absently answered the knock, busy thinking about the clean-up job Ralph was going to help him with that afternoon, the barn-slash-garage. It took Bernie so long to get to the door that the woman's hand was raised to knock again. She jumped, startled when it opened.

A little impatient, Bernie wasn't exactly sympathetic. *What did she expect? She's the one who knocked! Of course, he was going to open the door.*

"Hello," both she and Bernie said, simultaneously.

He relented with an embarrassed smile, barely able to keep from saying 'You owe me a coke,' as he would have in middle school.

There was nothing of middle school about this woman. Well, maybe she reminded him of his middle school teacher in Language Arts, Miss Artemis. *THAT* made him smile again, and his mind wandered until a small laugh recalled his attention to his doorway.

She was sure that the smile had been for her. The unexpected woman summoned her confidence and held up a plate covered with a pretty kitchen towel. "I brought you something to welcome you to the neighborhood."

She looked vaguely familiar, but then so many people had shown up – uninvited – to his impromptu bonfire not long ago, that *everyone* looked familiar. He hesitated, trying to place her. She definitely reminded him of someone... His distracted response, however unintentional, made her smile falter a little.

"Tina. Tina Meadows. I live just down the road a piece. I put my address on the bottom of the plate so you can return it." It was a little disconcerting to note that he hadn't even given her carefully chosen outfit a second look. And, since they were still standing at the door, and he hadn't reached out for the plate, she felt her chances of being invited in, dwindling.

"No hurry. I just enjoy baking and love to share. Blueberry muffins!" She added as she gave a little lift and flourish of the plate to entice him into at least looking down. She could put off the 'let's-get-to-know-each-other-better part of her agenda until he returned the plate.

Bernie was not usually this slow on the uptake. He had experienced a number of women wanting to console him after the death of his wife a year ago, but usually he *knew* them.

His younger stepbrother, Ralph, would be laughing himself sick if he were watching and listening. *You're slow, Bro.*

Bernie finally realized he still had not responded, at least, out loud. He sucked in his stomach, belatedly. "I'm sorry; I was just thinking about something else and then couldn't place you right away."

Oops.

He hoped his smile made up for accidentally telling her she was forgettable. "They look wonderful. I'll look forward to having them after supper."

She brightened at his genuine smile. "See you soon, then!" She wiggled her fingers in a little wave as she retreated back to the road.

Her high heels sank with each step into the ubiquitous sand, her arms outstretched for better balance. The ridiculous shoes were a better choice for a sidewalk, or a floor, anywhere but his yard. Surely, she would know that? Maybe she was going somewhere else, after, and didn't want to change shoes? Even as the thought went through his head, he was watching the interesting things that the strappy sandals did to her backside as she walked. The flippy little skirt of her yellow sundress barely covered what it needed to as it teased back and forth.

CHAPTER 2 SUNDAY

Ralph emerged from the depths of the barn with another armload of boxes. The bottoms were threatening to give way to the assorted metal stored in them. "I think your great uncle belonged to the Large-Heavy-Object-of-the-Month Club." He dropped them next to the last ones he had carried out.

Bernie was running a little behind Ralph in his sorting duties.

Ever organized, Ralph had designated a spot for "keep" and a spot for "donate" and had planned for "trash" to just get tossed into the back of his pick-up truck.

Bernie, however, had subdivided the "keep" pile into "definitely" and "maybe." The "donate" pile was now "I'll have to think about that" and "What the heck is that, anyway?" The truck only had a few old tires Ralph himself had tossed in.

While Ralph watched, Bernie reached into the truck bed and pulled out one of the tires.

"These make great little flower beds," Bernie commented, remembering some he had seen on a yard-DIY site.

"No, they don't," Ralph told him. Then he added the deadly red-neck sentiment, "That's a Yankee thing. Just plant stuff in the dirt in the ground, already."

"We don't have dirt – we have sand." Bernie gave him a sideways glance but reluctantly tossed the tire back into the truck bed.

He picked up a strange-looking white box, one of three. Ralph had put it in the "donate" pile. "What is this? It looks vaguely familiar."

"That's a beehive."

"Seriously?"

Ralph showed him how the frames pulled out.

"I should have bees."

Ralph laughed at him. "You're as bad as your great-uncle was. I've never seen so much junk."

"It was probably all in a lot better shape when he left for a few weeks' vacation thirty years ago. I remember being impressed with how bright and shiny everything was when I was a kid." He moved the bee boxes to the side of the barn. He would see about getting bees. Meanwhile, if he just left them out would some bees find them? Maybe...

"Sorry, man. Tough business, a stroke is. Half-alive for decades." Ralph cleared his throat after unnecessarily recapping the unfortunate event. He wasn't good at sentimental stuff.

Now, cleaning things out, *that* he was good at!

Bernie brushed the grease off what was presumably a random car part and then had to brush the grease off his hand onto a rag from his pocket. Unfortunately, he managed to get it all over his shorts while pulling out the rag. He grimaced. Of all the household chores he had learned since Betty died, he hated laundry the most. She was even more of an angel in his eyes, now.

"Everything was a lot bigger, then, too." Bernie looked back at the house – seriously in need of some tender-loving care.

"You'll be glad it isn't any bigger when we get started painting." Ralph pointed out.

The Sears House – Model 161 – ordered from a catalog and shipped from Chicago in about 1930 – was two-story but was dwarfed by the significantly newer barn/garage at the back of the lot. While various relatives had "borrowed" Uncle Sean's house over the years for Florida vacations, the intimidating barn had been ignored.

Bernie slapped his brother's shoulder "I'm hungry. Want a beer?"

"Whatever did you do to rate these?" Ralph asked as he bit into one of the muffins Bernie had set out to go with their late lunch.

"I'm not sure. Her name was Tina."

"I remember her from the bonfire."

"You do? I guess I just had other things on my mind." Bernie frowned. "Did I say or do anything to encourage her or anyone else?"

"Big brother, all you need to do is look in a woman's direction down here. There are twice as many women as men in our age group!"

"I'm not really interested yet." Bernie licked sauce off his fingers after catching some errant cheese from the meat-lovers' pizza and tossing it to land next to his cat, Patches. She gobbled it and meowed.

Ralph laughed at the cat. "You need a dog."

"Don't go there, Ralph."

Typical of brothers everywhere, Ralph couldn't let it go. "I'm just saying. You love animals and you had the best dog in the world. You know it, he knew it, and there will never be another one like him. But that doesn't mean you can't ever love another... dog." He cut himself off, uncomfortably. His little speech had somehow cut too close not only to the Golden Retriever Bernie had just lost a few months ago, but also to Bernie's late wife.

Bernie frowned and chose to ignore the whole thing – again. "I'm supposed to take Tina's plate back to her. The address is on the bottom of the plate. Now I'm going to feel weird about it. Are you sure she wasn't just being friendly?" He took a bite of the muffin, "maybe she's married."

Ralph heedlessly shoved the muffins off the plate onto the vinyl tablecloth and turned the plate over. "She was smart.

This way she's almost guaranteed to see you again. A married woman would have used a paper plate.

"Just down the road, looks about three or four lots away," Ralph commented. He wiggled his eyebrows, "I could take the plate back for you…"

"Would you? That would be great," Bernie sighed with relief.

"You really aren't interested? It's been quite a while since, you know, since you lost her." Ralph stumbled a little over the appropriate wording. He hadn't been overly fond of his sister-in-law, but he knew his brother's grief over her death was genuine.

"Just barely over a year," Bernie corrected. "Nothing wrong with Tina, I'm just not ready for anyone else, yet."

"We still have days of work ahead of us. How long do you want to work today?" Ralph pointedly looked at the time on his phone.

"I thought you didn't have anything going on this afternoon." Bernie asked bemusedly.

"Might as well return Tina's plate to her... and, since I'm going to, I have to clean up first."

"What will Heather think about that?"

"If she's jealous, she shouldn't have left me when I was, er, away."

Bernie shook his head at Ralph's reluctance to actually say "in jail." To be sure, it was not a chapter to be proud of, but it wasn't as if Bernie (and everyone else) didn't know where he'd been those few months. "And Miss Patty?"

Ralph couldn't help it. He laughed out loud. The idea of a romantic entanglement with that crotchety woman was just too funny. "Miss Patty is friend-zone, buddy. You think *you're* not interested; you should hear her on the subject."

Enough of *that* subject. "Tomorrow?" Bernie asked hopefully. He didn't mind a lot of work, but it was more fun with Ralph giving him a hard time about – well, about *everything*.

"You got it. I'll be here early," Ralph reached over to grab the plate, "I'll bring coffee and doughnuts to make up for leaving early today."

Bernie rubbed his stomach. "Probably not doughnuts," he had gained nearly ten pounds since moving here and hanging out with Ralph. "We'll still have most of these. Muffins aren't as fattening as doughnuts, are they? No frosting, anyway."

Big Foot and the Bentley

CHAPTER 3   MONDAY

The barn had apparently had nine lives. The huge interior had a couple of stalls with Dutch-split exterior doors, the kind where the top half can be open and the bottom half closed. They were on the left as you walked in and had long ago been latched and locked to the outside. The fenced-in area outside of them, a tiny corral, had long ago gone back to nature.

The area where tractors had probably been stored, to the right, had been given over to shelving and a concrete pad for working under a car. A pretty nice set-up for a shade-tree mechanic – without leaves, acorns, pine needles, etc., that a home mechanic had to cope with. Squirrels...

That was as far as he and Ralph had gotten yesterday. Most of the boxes and old furniture had come from the stalls and the back wall.

Today they were looking at a locked, barn-type set of hanging doors behind the mechanic shop. It sported a hefty-sized lock.

"Saw it off?" Ralph suggested.

"Good luck with that lock. I probably have a key to it inside the house."

In the habit of little brothers everywhere, "I'll bet I can get it off faster than you can find the key."

"You're on!" Bernie jogged back to the house. *When had he reverted to middle-school, interminably competing with his brothers?* He headed for the key hooks hanging on the wall, at the bottom of the inside stairs going up.

There were three sets of keys. It was a Master Lock. Master Lock keys say so, he thought. He grabbed all three rings and started going through them as he walked back out the door. Mature as the two men were, he still wanted to win. He tripped off the bottom step and lost his place on the first ring, started again. He stepped in a gopher hole and gave up. He would have to stand still while sorting the keys or risk a broken leg.

He had way too much to do to risk a broken leg.

A high-pitched whine and shriek came from the barn. Bernie hastily gathered up the keys into his fist again and ran for the barn.

Ralph had a beat-up circular saw and was ruining a blade as he leaned on the door to steady his arms against the bucking of the tool.

"That's cheating!" Bernie yelled above the racket.

Ralph heard him and laughed but didn't dare look up or he'd risk losing a hand.

Bernie didn't even bother finishing with the keys, just tossed them onto the workbench and watched his brother win the bet by cutting the latch, not the lock.

"What did I win, anyway?" Ralph asked as he tossed the lock to one side and wound the cord around the saw. He replaced it in the canvas pouch he'd fetched from his truck. "I'm sure there's a tool here that would have worked, but I had mine with me. Did your Uncle Sean even have battery-operated saws and drills thirty years ago?"

"Bragging rights," Bernie answered, "you won bragging rights." He surveyed the neat shelves and the array of electrical cords hanging down. "I doubt it. Elbow grease or electrical cords, it looks like. Did they even have battery powered tools back then?"

They worked well in tandem, as brothers often do. Bernie grabbed the hanging door on the right, while Ralph grabbed the one on the left. Both braced their feet on the floor as best they could and tried to slide their doors away from the middle.

"Come on, Man." Ralph gasped, "What's taking you so long?"

Bernie looked up at the rail the doors hung on and shook his head at the straw and string that littered the bar. "Me? I'm just taking it easy on *you*." His foot slipped on the wood floor. He turned and braced to push instead of pull.

"I already" Ralph's hand slipped, and he cursed as his knuckles tore on the wood, "beat you once today; do your worst!" He put his knuckles in his mouth, pulled them out to look at them and cursed again.

"You kiss our Mama with that mouth?" Bernie got out in spurts as his door started to slide.

Ralph laughed and slid to the floor, chuckling at the thought Bernie telling on him to their mother.

Bernie stood and stared. He heard, rather than saw, Ralph scramble up to turn and stand next to him.

Ralph let out a long whistle.

"Trust you to ruin the moment," Bernie growled. *Why could everyone in the known universe whistle except him?*

"Sorry."

Dim light filtered between the blinds over the single window. The baby blue paint and the dark blue top were dusty; the distinctive square grill had lost a little of its shine. The "B" hood ornament and the round lights proclaimed it to be from the sixties.

"Wow."

"Have you got the title to that?" Ralph asked.

"Not that I know of; but you've seen what I still have to go through. Makes sense, though, that the title would be here somewhere. I wonder if it runs?"

"I'd bet 'yes.'"

"You would. No bets on this. This is serious." Bernie shoved a rolling tool-stool out of the way so he could walk around it to the driver's side.

It didn't roll and Bernie tripped over it. *What was it with simply walking all of a sudden?"*

Ralph came up behind him and went to wipe the dust off of the hood. Bernie grabbed his wrist. "Water. Rubbing the dust and dirt off scratches the paint. Always wash it off with running water."

It was a mark of Ralph's awe that he didn't even argue.

"What do you know about old cars?" Ralph asked his big brother. It seemed sometimes that Bernie knew just about everything.

"Not much. But I'll bet there's a car club here, somewhere. And, I'll bet they knew Uncle Sean..."

CHAPTER 4 WEDNESDAY

Catherine flipped over an Ace of Spades. "Twenty-one."

The game they played changed with where they played. Bernie had de facto replaced Pete in the weekly card games. Married life had caught up with Pete and he was happier at home in the evenings now.

Patty fetched another round of drinks from inside and flipped on additional lights, crisscrossed under the vendor tent that sheltered her patio.

Her rooster crowed and Patty cringed.

"Why the face?" Bernie asked her.

"It's kind of late. I should have already had them covered. I hear from the neighbors when Meanie gets noisy at night." She hastened over to draw a dark tarp over the chicken run.

"They're getting kind of big for that space," Bernie commented idly.

"And you have a better suggestion?" Patty snapped at him. "Space is kind of at a premium, here."

"He didn't…" Ralph tried to smooth things over, but Bernie interrupted him.

"I didn't mean that as a criticism, Miss Patty. It was just an observation.

What is your plan for them? What do you do in the cold weather?"

Catherine chimed in. "She put them in crates and took them inside the camper."

Patty glared at her.

Apparently, that was a touchy subject.

Ever the peacemaker, Ralph changed topics. "Did I tell you about the car Bernie found in his barn?"

"He has a barn?" Catherine asked and chewed her bottom lip, trying to remember the one evening she had spent there – the night of the bonfire.

"Great big thing, behind the clearing where he had the fire," Patty supplied. "Needs paint," she commented. "What kind of car?"

"A 1961 S2 Mulliner Continental Drophead Coupe."

"Speak English," groused Patty.

"Cool old car," interpreted Catherine.

Ralph grinned and clarified for the women, "A Bentley." He raised an eyebrow at his brother. "You've done some research! Did you find out anything about this one specifically?"

"Not yet. I identified it from the book in the glove box. I'm half afraid to even try to clean it up." Bernie said in a rare admission among friends. "I just stand in the doorway and look at it."

"Don't tell me you haven't looked it up online. How much is it worth?" Ralph asked.

Bernie hedged. "Their prices at auction vary widely."

Patty pulled out her phone. "A Bentley what?"

The men ignored her.

"You said 1961? Coupe?"

Ralph still ignored her and pressed his brother. "You took a couple of days off from cleaning the barn in order to research it. Surely, you've found more than that.

Speaking of taking time off, we need to do something with the piles in your yard. It's supposed to rain on Sunday."

"I covered them with tarps. They'll be okay until next week. I've got stuff to do Thursday, and I found a car club that meets on Friday evenings downtown."

"That one I see sometimes by the pizza place?" Ralph asked.

"Every Friday. The President is out of town for a few days but was monitoring the group's page. She told me she'd be there at the next meeting if I show up."

"Did you tell her why you wanted to meet with them?" Ralph asked.

"The president of the car club is a woman?" Patty was surprised; then she found what she was looking for. "Holy crap. That car could be worth a quarter-million."

"Not it's not. I did find one that sold for $189,000, though."

"I should be charging you for helping in the barn! Isn't your birthday next week?

That's a heck of a birthday present!" Ralph asked him.

Catherine suddenly started paying attention again. Birthdays she was conversant with, cool old cars, not so much.

"I don't have birthdays, anymore," Bernie asserted.

"Nonsense. If you don't tell me what kind of cake you want, you'll get a mincemeat pie." Catherine announced, winking at Patty.

Bernie lost his grin, "I don't know about that..."

"You'd better say, then!"

"How about a blueberry pie? I'll bring you the blueberries." There was a hopeful note in his voice.

Ralph recalled the muffins, "Remind me to tell you about Tina, Bro."

"Tina who?" Dr. Catherine asked.

"Never-you-mind. You'll probably meet her soon," Ralph told her.

CHAPTER 5   THURSDAY

"Do you need a container?" The woman peered around her counter to see if he had one.

Her dress, her apron, and even her eyes were blueberry colored. Bernie wondered if it was intentional. Weren't there colored contacts now? Then wondered if her apron was orange when pumpkins were ready. The sudden vision of pumpkin-orange eyes freaked him out a little. He shook his head. "Yes. I'm sorry; I'm afraid it didn't even occur to me to bring something to put them in."

"Not a problem, here's a bucket, and when it's full or you're done, we'll empty it into a plastic sack to weigh." She handed him a small, black bucket with a wire handle. "It's picked pretty clean right here. Go all the way back or over a few rows in either direction. Keep an eye out for snakes." She winked at him.

What was that for? Did she wink at everyone? Did she mean she was only teasing about the snakes? He looked down at his feet warily. Boots would have been better than sandals. It wasn't that he was afraid of snakes – exactly. One should just be wary around them…

There were only a few people picking that early. He followed someone out of the sheet metal shelter.

It was just a coincidence that the person he followed was a young woman.

Who wouldn't have followed her? She was attractive, not that he'd noticed. But, now that he had, he was uncomfortable.

She just looked confident and experienced, he told himself.

He was not confident, nor experienced – with blueberries. He didn't want to look creepy, so he looked down.

Better to look down, anyway. Snakes, he reminded himself…

The girl entered a row about seven or eight down. He followed slowly and took the next one. Then he started actually looking at the waist-high bushes. He'd never picked blueberries before and was somewhat startled to see how many of them there were on each plant. He started picking the darkest, first on one side of the row and then the other, and progressed away from the parking area. He turned at the end, skipped a row, and headed back; repeating his picking pattern.

Several rows farther down, the bushes looked different. When he got close, he could see several bushes looked like someone had just closed his hand around the main stem and pulled upwards, stripping the bushes of all the berries, ripe or not, and most of the leaves.

King Kong came to mind. Then Faye Ray came to mind.

Hmm.

One smaller bush was bent double and lying on the ground, the heavy sand, still wet from an early morning storm, was holding it down. Reaching down, Bernie brushed off most of the heavy sand and pulled it back upright. It sagged but stood. It was the last row of blueberries, fortunately, since his bucket was full.

Picking was hypnotic, he thought, always just one more off the next plant, then another one just out of reach...

The next row over was peach trees. They weren't ripe, but several had bites taken out of them and lay on the ground.

He left the carefully tended rows and stepped carefully into the shadow of the adjacent woods. He sensed rather than saw a trail as he ventured deeper. A rustle made him stop and look frantically around for a snake.

A few more steps and he discovered he could see the outline of his barn. A decrepit shed was another direction, and bog stretched out in front and into the distance the other way. Creepers and palmettos filled the gaps between the trees. Muscadine grapevines cascaded. It was beautiful and wild.

He nearly spilled the bucket trying to navigate back. Having already passed that way, his caution deserted him and he tripped on a passion flower vine.

There was a heavy, wet, smell in the air. It kind of left an aftertaste when he absently popped a blueberry in his mouth.

"It looks like something was eating on your bushes and trees down that way." He gestured toward the peach trees when he got back to the counter. "Do you know what it was? A bear? It looked big."

"Did you actually see something?" She stopped and stared at him.

"No, no. I was just going by the damage. I have five acres the other side of that boggy area and the woods. I just moved in. I was worried about my cat, mostly."

She resumed bagging his berries, but wouldn't meet his eyes. "I keep my cats inside at night. Our bears aren't very big, but they're there and there are other things that roam at night. That'll be $25.00 please." She took his card.

"I ate some."

"Everyone does. Cost of doing

business, unless you come back and hand me an empty bucket," she smiled.

"What kinds of things roam around at night?"

"Oh, snakes, panthers, coyotes, raccoons."

Bernie laughed. "Somehow, I can't see a coyote climbing a peach tree or stripping a berry bush!"

She just smiled at him, handed his card back, and turned to a man who had come in behind him.

The conversation was over.

Bernie was looking down into his plastic sack as he turned to leave and almost ran into a woman who was entering, carrying a huge plastic baker's tray of wrapped baked goods. He hastily shifted his bag to his left forearm and reached to take the tray from her. "I'm sorry. I wasn't paying attention. Let me help."

For a moment he thought he was going to have to wrestle for it. She, apparently reluctant to accept help, and he, too well-trained by his stepmom to not help, were at an impasse.

"Thank you! I'm just headed for that counter, there." She gave in and gestured toward several clear plastic display cases. He had overlooked them before, probably because they were all empty.

"Wow! Do they sell out of your goods every day?"

The bakery-lady (plump, sweet smile, smelled like cinnamon) laughed at him. "Don't I wish! I have to come and get anything left over in the evening. If we leave it out all night, it just invites trouble."

"Raccoons? I've heard they have nimble fingers."

"Those, too, but…" she was cut off by Berry-woman.

"I was just explaining to our guest about coyotes and 'coons." She gave the bakery lady a warning look. "It's surprising the damage they can do – to the bushes and trees — isn't it?"

"Uh, yes. Yes, it is amazing." Bakery-lady turned toward him again, "Thank you for helping me; I have it from here." She reached over and plucked a plastic-wrapped bear claw from her stack and handed it to Bernie.

That conversation was *also* over!

CHAPTER 6 FRIDAY

"I didn't know your uncle Sean, but

my dad probably did," Myrna answered. "Hey, Dad! Come here a minute."

An old guy wearing a baseball cap with an Army logo on it perked up when she called. He had been headed toward a group of folding chairs, carrying a take-out tray from the pizza place. "Hold your horses, Young'un." He distributed the drinks to the other men, stuck his in the cupholder of the one empty chair, and turned toward them.

The man had a limp and was easily twenty years Bernie's senior. Bernie felt bad about making him walk over to them and stood to at least meet him halfway.

Kevin waved him back down and took an empty chair next to his daughter under the myrtle tree. "It's not often I get invited over here, anymore – I have to take advantage."

Myrna made a rude noise.

Bernie glanced around at the several groups of car owners and aficionados gathered under different trees on the edges of the parking lot.

"Assigned seating?" Bernie asked, lightly.

"Nah. Except for me and my husband. We sit here because he parks the trailer here and plugs in the music over there." Myrna pointed at an outlet on the side of the building. "He's gone to get the trailer out of their shed, now." She gestured vaguely toward the back of the building.

"What do you two kids need help with?" Kevin raised his bushy, gray eyebrows in question.

Bernie laughed. It had been a long time since anyone called him a kid. Uncle Sean had technically been the patriarch of the family for many years but had been long unable to address anyone. "I was hoping to meet someone who knew my great uncle, Sean Murphy. "I'm Bernie Murphy." He stuck out his hand to shake.

The older man shook his hand enthusiastically. "Sean Murphy, you say? Good to hear the name again! Nice to meet you, Bernie! We only found out a few years back what had happened to him. For the longest time, he was simply here one Friday, and we never saw the old coot again."

Bernie nodded and accepted culpability in not notifying anyone. "After he had the stroke, we were all hoping he would bounce back. Then he had another, and thirty years from the first one, here we are. I was just telling your daughter that he passed away and left me his home."

The man and his daughter looked at each other and Myrna cleared her throat. "Are you here just by chance, then, at the Classic Car Club, I mean? Are you a classic car fan?"

"Funny you should ask that. There's a car in the barn…"

Kevin caught his breath and held it.

Myrna gave him a funny look.

Bernie stopped talking.

"Well, get after it man. What kind of

car is it?" Kevin demanded.

"It's a Bentley." There, it was out. These folk knew more about the car than he did. They might even know what it was worth.

Kevin had his phone out and was texting a-mile-a-minute.

"Dad, be careful. We only know one side of the story."

Bernie looked from one to the other. "What story?"

Myrna took a deep breath. "Another man in the club claimed he asked Sean to store his car for him. When Sean disappeared, Harold claimed Sean had stolen his car."

"Why didn't he report it to the police?"

"Actually, it would have been the Sheriff. He did try to report it, but Harold couldn't produce the title, and, well, he was known for gambling. A search of the title records didn't even show one in his name.

It didn't show one in Sean's name, either. Long story short, no one in law enforcement was much interested."

"We all saw the car, one time, before then. Harold was new here, and brought it to show it off, once." Kevin put in. "It was a rough summer, that year, lots of storms. We started having poker and beer get-togethers whenever a storm canceled us here.

"Drank lots of beer that year."

Myrna picked up the story. "Not long after that, Harold had a heart attack and died. His widow has always claimed it was losing the car that did it. Twenty- twenty-five years ago?"

Kevin shook his head. He glanced over at the drink he had waiting at his chair. Myrna saw him and walked over to get the cup.

He took it gratefully. "Thank you, my dear." He sipped through the straw.

"His widow's kind of gone off the

deep end," Kevin said after a long draw.

"Now, Dad, that's unkind."

"Okay, she's become unhinged."

"That wasn't exactly better," chided Myrna.

"Her ragtop doesn't quite latch," Kevin grinned, "Her fuel filter is a little clogged..."

Myrna laughed. To Bernie, she added, "She was arrested a couple of times. It seems her medication makes her a little unstable."

"Downright violent, you mean. Ran that one neighbor clean out of Florida. The Sheriff took her guns away from her after her sister-in-law died and she threatened to kill her brother. Terrible scene. Always felt sorry for the boy. Thank heavens for his cousin taking them in."

One of the other guys from Kevin's group had meandered over to see what was going on. He only caught the last comment but knew exactly who they were talking about. "You mean Caroleen, don't you?"

"Yeah, Connor, this is Bernie Murphy. Bernie, Connor. It seems Sean left Bernie his house – and his car."

Bernie thought it was interesting to note that no further explanation was necessary. Sean must have been a legend.

"Did he, now?" Connor stroked his impressive white beard. "You don't say. Does Caroleen know? We all thought he'd driven the car up north when he left. It's here?"

"She, Caroleen, was on the phone with my wife just a week ago. Now she claims she's on her deathbed and can't afford to die. She said Harold spent all their savings on the car and they were supposed to be buried together in it."

Bernie was aghast. "Is that even legal?" Questions regarding the ownership of the car took second place to *this* revelation. "I mean, wouldn't the health department have something to say about that? What cemetery would agree to a hole that size?" The whole idea was mind-boggling.

"If you have a family cemetery…" Myrna started.

"But that would be out in the country," Bernie interrupted. "Don't most of those homes have wells?" The idea of pumping water from a well near such a burial site almost made him gag.

"I think you're supposed to be cremated, first…" Kevin started to explain.

"What about the petroleum products that would leach out of the car?" Bernie bounced from one objection to another, out loud, as each one occurred to him.

He stood up to leave. Kevin and Myrna looked at each other. They were better off dropping it for now.

"It was nice meeting you," Bernie murmured as he turned and left the parking area, walking past the man hooking up a sound system.

Bernie was shaking his head as he

pulled out the keys to his Mustang. *Even without the objections he'd already brought up, bury a car worth that much money? Talk about a burial plan...*

Myrna's husband waved at him, but Bernie didn't see him or look back.

Kevin answered his daughter's accusing look defensively. "I wasn't texting Caroleen, by the way. If you'd stopped to think about it, can you imagine her actually texting? She doesn't even have a cell phone. She's lucky to eat most weeks."

Myrna looked apologetic. "You're right. Who were you texting, then?"

"A friend of mine at the Sheriff's Department, Dan. He asked me about the car recently, because Caroleen cornered his wife about it at a church function not long ago."

"Not long ago? How long ago?" She narrowed her eyes suspiciously. "*At* a church function? What function? No one's seen Caroleen since the pandemic started."

Kevin mumbled an answer and stood to make his way back to his own chair, vacating the one saved for Myrna's husband.

Myrna wasn't going to let it go, "*how recently?*" She called after him.

He knew she wouldn't let up and raised his voice just a little to repeat himself, "ten years, more or less."

Myrna rolled her eyes.

CHAPTER 7 SATURDAY

"Problem is, it might not actually be mine. I have to find the title if it's here."

"Don't they say possession is nine-tenths of the law?" Ralph stepped around him to look at the car one more time. It was a hard thing to take your eyes off of. "We need to push it out of there so we can clean it up."

"I want to find the title, first." Bernie looked around.

There wasn't much else in the room. A few shelves had some boxes. There was one of those file boxes, the metal kind and the lid flipped up and back. *That would just be too easy...*

It was.

There was some maintenance information. "Needs an oil change – it's been a while," Bernie said wryly.

Ralph let out a snort. "Well, is it in there?"

"Nah. I guess I'll have to go through the office upstairs. I've been meaning to do it, anyway." *Dreading doing it, was more to the point. Maybe if he opened the curtains up there it wouldn't be so gloomy. Who wants to spend a warm Florida day inside?*

"I'm not ready to get it out, yet," Bernie turned Ralph down as he gestured to the car. "But, hey, you'll be the first to know when I am."

"Did I tell you about Tina, by the way?" Ralph asked. "I think she was a little put out that I showed up with the plate she left you. But you know my charm, I won her over.

"She's widowed but lives with her uncle, Carl, and his teenage son. Or, do they live with her, I haven't figured it out yet. Tina's husband was killed by a poacher for poaching in the other guy's territory, *his* alligators. Carl's some kind of mechanic.

Kid's a nerd.

"She was wearing a swimsuit top with shorts." Ralph leered, "Her legs are a mile long."

Unbidden, Bernie recalled those tan legs just below the sassy yellow sundress.

He was mourning, not dead.

"Are you taking her out, then?" Bernie asked.

"Next Friday. Taking her to dinner and a show at the theatre by the old courthouse in Inverness."

The two men were walking past the garden. Bernie picked up two big bird feeders and put them to one side. Then he pulled the tarp back over the 'donate' pile while Ralph pulled another one over the 'recycle' pile. Most of the 'keep' pile was already back on shelves they built earlier that day.

Bernie handed one feeder to Ralph and carried the other one to the old clothesline pole near the fire pit. He hung one up and Ralph hung his on the other side.

"I'll get birdseed, want to come?"

Ralph gave a sigh at the pile in the back of his truck. "Nah. Next time. I got stuff to do. The landfill is closed today, I guess I'll just have to drive around with this mess in the back for a couple of days.

"Makes me feel like that show on TV when we were kids. You know, the one they can't show reruns of anymore."

"Yeah, I know the one." Bernie gave a snort. It's kind of funny how so many old shows are not allowed anymore.

"Would it be rude if I sent the blueberries home with you to Catherine?" Bernie abruptly changed the subject.

"Why? There's no reason to avoid her; she's not interested in you."

"Would you PLEASE get your mind off that track," Bernie begged. "Never mind, I'll take them over."

"Good Lord Almighty!" Dr Catherine gasped.

Bernie frowned down into his sack, looking for a snake, lizard or even a palmetto bug. "What?"

"Just how many pies do you want?"

"Did I get a little carried away? There was always just one more bush in front of me with another few berries on top... I really had no idea how many you'd need..."

"I get it. I get it." She waved at him to stop his explanation, "I'm in the mood to bake. I can make you blueberry pancakes you can heat up in your toaster. I can also make some blueberry tarts, some muffins, and still have enough for two pies – Florida style."

"One for the freezer." Bernie supplied from his childhood memories.

"Why don't we save the tarts for cards on Wednesday?" Bernie suggested. "Do you have room in your freezer for the extra pie?" He eyed the trailer behind where she held court on her patio. It was a mansion of trailers. It was easily the longest one he'd ever seen off of a sales lot. There was a bedroom at either end, each with its own bathroom. There was a sitting room and kitchen in the middle.

A ramp led to Catherine's door in the rear. Hers was the biggest of the bedrooms, the master, and had its own sitting area.

"No worries. It has a full-size refrigerator. You don't want two?"

"I thought you should keep it for your trouble. I haven't met your nephew, yet, but I figure JJ might like pie."

He hadn't met JJ, yet, but he had heard stories…

"You haven't met him yet?" Catherine frowned. "How has that happened?"

"Well, we're usually at Ralph's or Patty's. The one time we played here he was gone to a revival in Georgia somewhere."

"We can have cards here, this week. I'll see if JJ is going to be around. Between preaching at two churches and now doing counseling at the free clinic in Beverly Hills two afternoons a week, he's hard to keep track of."

"That's not necessary. We could have cards at my place."

"Oh, wait. What was I thinking? No wonder you haven't met JJ. We play on Wednesdays, and he does Wednesday church at the other mobile home park.

"We'll have it here anyway. I insist!"

Bernie was never sure what to expect from Dr Catherine or her eccentric friend, Patty. "Nothing special, now. No balloons or to-do, just pie, now," he warned her.

"And whipped cream! You have to have whipped cream with blueberry pie."

Big Foot and the Bentley

CHAPTER 8 SUNDAY

Bernie surveyed the mess.

The bag of birdseed he had eventually settled on, with the help of a twelve-year-old customer service agent wearing a wedding ring, (*how old did you have to be to get married in Florida, anyway?*) was now scattered all over the garden plot by the back of his barn. It looked like something sharp had cut the plastic, net bag. A knife? A claw? What had big, sharp claws and would be interested in sunflower seeds? His mind went to bears again. He pictured a fat bear rolling around in ecstasy - areas of seed was pressed deeply into the dirt and sand by something heavy. Bear cubs?

He'd have to get a metal trashcan with a tight lid and put it inside the barn. He gathered the loose edges of the tear and picked up what was left of the bag to haul inside.

Then he saw the bee boxes – destroyed.

"Dispatch."

"My name's Bernie Murphy."

"Oh, yes, I remember you. What can we do for you?"

"Well, it's kind of strange. Either someone is purposely vandalizing my property, or there's a wild animal running around here."

"I heard about your car, but Caroleen doesn't get out much, anymore, and claims she's on her deathbed. But we doubt that because she's still alive enough to call in at least a couple of times a month with some complaint or another. Can you think of anyone else who might be vandalizing you?"

Bernie couldn't believe that apparently – everyone – knew about the car.

"No. I'd never even heard of her before Friday, and don't know that many other people, yet. What about an animal? Have there been reports?"

"If you're talking about the Swamp Ape..."

Bernie could almost see her roll her eyes at him. He hadn't thought about the Florida Big Foot in ages. Did people still talk about them? "I don't think so. Unless you have had sightings recently?" *It was something big, after all.*

The dispatcher laughed. "Once a week. Especially each year when the festival starts to advertise. I'll make a report and have someone stop by early next week. Take pictures for me."

Bernie slid his phone back into his

pocket after taking a few photos. Somehow the tiny screen didn't give justice to the depressed areas. Either the picture was just of the seeds, or if you wanted to get the whole rolling-around-print thing, you were too far away to see the seeds pressed into the ground. The bee boxes looked to be history. Well, maybe he could fix them...

Bernie stopped at the door to the barn and opened the simple latch. He needed better security. He also needed insurance.

It was Sunday – the farm store it was – security first.

He bought a metal trash can, bought more birdseed, and bought a couple more bird feeders. He bought a security light with a camera set-up. Then he bought a new latch for the barn door. He had found the keys to the Master Lock and would use it. If the outside door was locked, he wasn't too concerned about fixing the latch on the inside doors that Ralph had destroyed.

Who was he kidding? He went back

for one, and another lock.

There was a banana peel on the floor of the barn, a *banana* peel. He didn't have any bananas.

Someone had gotten into the barn, stood here and looked at his car, eating a banana.

A slow burn went through him. Then common sense. Maybe Ralph had come over for some reason. That would be okay. He tried to think of anyone else he might allow. Maybe Pete? There was something inherently likable and trustworthy about the guy.

No one else, though.

He was repairing latches and locks until late in the night.

Big Foot and the Bentley

CHAPTER 9 MONDAY

"What do you mean, 'No'?"

"I'm sorry, we can't insure any vehicle worth more than $100,000."

"What happens if the barn burns down? Is it covered under my household insurance?"

"No. If it separately insurable, it has to be insured separately."

"But you're telling me it's not insurable."

"Just not through us." She added as

an afterthought, "or any of the other major carriers..."

Bernie didn't even listen to the rest of what she had to say. When she stopped talking, he realized she was waiting for an answer to something he hadn't even heard.

"Thanks, anyway." Whatever she wanted, he was no longer interested. He stepped out into the sunshine and logged onto social media. He messaged Myrna. "Where do you guys get insurance for your vehicles? How about a mechanic?"

His stomach rumbled and he realized he had fed Patches and forgotten to fix his own breakfast. He looked both ways down the neighboring street – the 'old retail center' of town. There was a Tea House with healthy, light sandwiches, low-sodium chips, and herb tea. Or there was a coffee shop that presented a more manly air, and probably specialized in sugar, cinnamon, butter and cream, and carbs to hold them all together.

Manly location it was.

He was holding his cinnamon roll and waiting for his mocha coffee when Bakery-lady came in with yet another tray of sweets.

"I should have known these were yours!" He smiled at her, and she grinned back.

"One of my best locations. I remember you from the U-Pick Berry Café. My name's Hattie, by the way."

"Bernie Murphy. Do you have time for coffee?"

She looked at him speculatively.

He noted the ring on her finger. "No ulterior motive, just new in town. I see you're married."

"Just a minute." She finished checking in the order with the barista, and he handed her what was apparently a customary coffee order on the house.

Hattie tilted the empty tray against her chair and sat across from him at one of the tiny tables. He had already devoured half of his roll.

"I'm glad you like them – they're my specialty."

He swallowed the bite he had taken as she sat down.

"So, where are you from, Bernie Murphy?"

"Most recently, Arizona, but I lived here many years ago."

"I imagine it has changed a lot."

"More people, less wildlife."

"If this is about the other day at the Berry Place..."

"It's okay. I've just had something large making a mess back by my barn. No one wants to talk about what might be doing it."

"They aren't animals, you know." Hattie frowned. "They have to be smart or they'd be captured, tortured, wired up, and cut into."

Bernie looked suitably horrified. Whether at her leap of logic, or the very idea, was his own business.

"I've heard of a new family nesting – or settling – in the bog near the Berry Place. What have you seen?"

He considered the question seriously. She deserved a straight answer for even talking to him. "What might be footprints? Something tore into my birdseed and demolished a few bee boxes."

Now she looked horrified – at the destruction of endangered bees or the stings her cryptids might have suffered?

He reassured her quickly, "no bees. I hadn't gotten around to ordering any, yet."

"The hominids aren't a real popular topic around here. You should be careful when you ask about them. If you get a picture, I'd like to see it. With all the new cameras around, it's only a matter of time." She pulled a card out of her pocket and passed it to him. "I gotta go. Nice talking to you!"

A ding on his phone told him he had a message. Myrna had typed back "Llewellyn's of London. I imagine you're priced out of the local carriers...

Bernie snorted. *Yeah, he was, apparently.*

He pulled up a number he found online – they had a branch in Miami.

A carefully modulated voice answered the number. "Yes. We do insure antique, show quality, vehicles. I assume you have the title, registration, and an appraisal?"

Well, that conversation was also at an end. For now.

CHAPTER 10   TUESDAY

"I don't like bananas, Bro."

"Well, who do we know who does?"

"Like everyone, except us? Why?"

"Someone was in my barn, eating a banana and looking at the car. He dropped a banana peel."

"Magilla Gorilla comes to mind. Sorry. I know you're serious. I don't know. It does sound like you need to replace that lock, and maybe upgrade the outside door latch."

"Did all that Sunday night," Bernie volunteered. "What do you know about the Swamp Ape or Florida Big Foot?"

"Not as much as I would like to know. Big bucks in crazy people, nowadays. Festival coming up down south."

Bernie grunted at Ralph's cheeky answers.

Ralph had real concerns, though. "Seriously, have you managed insurance yet? That woman you were talking about sounds like trouble. She has a brother? And cousins?"

"I did call in a report, both one for some damage in the garden area and again regarding the banana." He hadn't shared the Big-Foot theory regarding the birdseed with Ralph. "They were less than impressed over the banana peel. I'm working on the insurance…"

CHAPTER 11   WEDNESDAY

When Bernie arrived at Catherine's, the lights under her awning were on. Music played inside but came through the screens at just the right decibel. He knew that station on cable, it was his kind of music. Southern gospel with a healthy mixture of classic country. He had walked over, expecting beer to be involved in his birthday/cards party.

Pete and Doris were there as well. Both of them sat on his ubiquitous gold golf cart truck with his cat on the seat between them. For Doris, the transportation helped with her mobility issues. For Pete, it saved time – as the maintenance person, he spent a LOT of time running back and forth across the park.

"Happy Birthday! We thought we'd start with pie and presents and play cards after." Doris was holding a foil-wrapped baking tray of some kind with a bow on top. Pete had a gallon jug with a bow on the handle.

Patty had a small box in her lap. "We're waiting for Ralph, as usual."

"I'm here, I'm here." Ralph came around the corner.

"Pie or presents, first?" Catherine asked.

"You weren't supposed to bring me anything!" Bernie groused good-naturedly. As much as he was dismayed by the attention, it was nice to have friends willing to celebrate with him. Last year's birthday had been a lonely affair.

"Pie, first." Pete nodded approval. Doris looked as though she was going to say something silly like, 'just a small piece' but looked at her new husband's face and just shook her head in resignation. Fruit was a good thing.

Patty handed Doris her plate and pointed out "Could be worse, could have been double chocolate cake with fudge icing and rocky-road ice cream…"

Pete laughed into the spoon of whipped cream he was about to eat and it sprayed his cat – who calmly licked it off.

The pie was every bit as good as Bernie had thought it would be, and he told Dr Catherine that several times.

"JJ ate a piece earlier from the other pie and said, 'Thank you.' He is interested in your car and wants to meet you – just don't try to sell it to him. All I could remember was that it was baby-blue, a Bentley, and really old and expensive." Dr Catherine shared. "If you don't care, he'd like to see it. Can I tell him he can drop by?

I'd make him call, first."

"I'll bring beer if I can come, too." Pete volunteered.

There was no mistaking Doris' disapproval that time. "Pop. Diet, or Sweet Tea, artificial sweetener." She was attempting to derail the high-calorie beer.

"Sure, why not? Like Catherine said, just call to make sure I'm home." Bernie basked in the warm, friendly atmosphere.

Doris started to get up to hand him her present. Bernie scrambled to get up and take it so she didn't have to put weight on her bandaged legs. "This is heavy!"

"It should be! It's my special lasagna! I froze it and cut it into squares and put them back in the pan so you can heat up one at a time or however many you want!"

"Are you sure you're happily married to that lug next to you?"

Doris' complexion turned a pretty pink and Pete reached over to put a proprietary hand on her pretty flowered skirt.

"This," Pete announced, "is my special rust-remover. Ralph says you have a lot of really good tools over there that just need some TLC and my rust-remover." He handed the jug to Bernie. "It just takes a little. I wrote the directions on the bottle. I'd give you the recipe, but I'd have to kill you."

"Is that concoction what happened to your hair?" Bernie asked and put a protective hand over his slowly-growing-out pate.

"I've got more hair than you ever did." Pete declared amiably and falsely.

Patty handed Bernie a box, next, and Ralph got up and left.

"Where you going?"

"Just open the box," instructed Patty. "He'll be back."

It was wrapped with brightly colored pages from a magazine, and a new ribbon. He tore them off and pried off the lid of a small plastic container. IT was stuffed with dog-owner paraphernalia. There was a new red harness, a long leash, a package of poop-bags, and two each food and water dishes. Ralph was coming around the corner with a squirming, light-colored, smallish-sized dog in one arm and a huge bag of dog-food under the other.

"Ralph…" Bernie started to vent some justified anger at him. He frowned right up until Ralph dropped the wriggling pup into his lap. Big, brown, adoring eyes met his.

"Well?" Patty demanded, "Ralph and I went together."

He looked down into the happy face that had yet to make a noise and got a lick on his chin. "That's enough of that, young man!" He tried to check but wound up asking. "Boy? Girl?"

"Boy."

"Does he have a name?"

"He's a rescue; the sign said 'Pierre'

on the crate he was living in."

"He is NOT a Pierre. What is he, exactly?"

"He's a cocker-slash-poodle," Ralph explained.

"He doesn't look like any Cockapoo I've ever seen... His coat's wrong and he's not very big and he's the wrong color."

Patty chimed in, "Probably one reason he was still with the breeder at almost a year old. He got the alternate genes to a Cockapoo. I'd say he's a Cock-a-doodle, instead!"

"Forgiven?" Ralph asked with a little trepidation.

"Oh, just tell him it was my fault, already. If he never speaks to me again, he'll at least still have his brother!" Patty declared.

Bernie's throat threatened to close up on him and his usually quick mind struggled for a snappy come-back.

"If I stop speaking to you, Miss Patty, how are we going to bid at Pinochle?"

CHAPTER 12   THURSDAY

Ralph, Pete, and a stranger in a white, short-sleeve, button-down shirt and white slacks, piled out of Ralph's truck into his driveway as Bernie scarfed down the last of the cereal in his bowl. 'Calling ahead' in the west meant just that, giving you time to prepare for company. 'Calling ahead' here meant 'we're on the way.' Ralph had only called five minutes ago. Bernie had barely had time to feed Patches, pour dog food into a new bowl for – whatever his name was going to be – and get a bowl of oats for himself.

Bernie stayed in the window to watch them come up the walk. His new pup bounced between trying to eat his cereal and trying to see what was happening at the front door at the same time. Kibble was all over the floor.

Patches was in hiding.

It amused Bernie that the guy in white had an uncanny resemblance to Colonel Sanders of fried chicken fame. He had to be Dr Catherine's womanizing nephew; hadn't Patty even referred to him as Colonel Sanders, once?

He heard Pete's fake-petulant voice coming through the front screen door. "I have to work to get to see it!"

"I hadn't considered charging admission, but I'm beginning to think I should," Bernie declared. "You must be JJ?" Bernie held out his hand and the man smiled and shook it. Puppy bounced up and down. JJ backed up.

"Very glad to meet you, Suh. My lady aunt has had much to say on your behalf."

"They could help stack the 'donate' pile in my truck, in lieu of admission, now that the bed's finally empty again," Ralph suggested hopefully. "Unless, of course all of *that* pile has migrated back inside the barn!"

"I just moved a *few* things," Bernie allowed, taking Ralph's suggestion as a bona-fide offer. "Helping with that stuff would be great. Thanks!"

"Plus, it would keep you from appropriating more of it!" Ralph gestured to the pile to be moved as he led them back to the barn. Pete just nodded. JJ looked at the dusty heap with an air of distaste.

Bernie undid the lock and Ralph

opened the door with a proprietary air that made Bernie smile. The men trooped through, with JJ turning sideways to go through without brushing the door or having to use his hand to push it wider. Bernie was amused. It was amusing, yes, but also annoying. He and Ralph had just spent a week cleaning and organizing the barn. Yes, there was lingering dust in the air, and they hadn't even looked in the loft (the built-in ladder was a little scary) but overall, it was one of the cleanest barns he'd ever been in.

White, Bernie snorted.

Puppy followed Bernie as if he'd been doing it since he was born. Any lingering worry about him running off was dying out. "Good dog!"

The expressions of the two visitors made him – almost – decide to keep the car. He was already getting the inkling that getting a title, registering it and then paying for insurance was going to be a nightmare. Then there was the inevitable maintenance to be done – rubber had most likely rotted.

He hadn't found any rodents, yet, but he was sure wires would need replacing. The fuel system would have to be cleaned out. There was no way he could even remotely justify keeping it – except for the looks on his friends' faces.

He wondered idly if anyone in the downtown car club could afford it? A coastal community invariably included under-the-radar wealthy residents. Homosassa, Crystal River, Yankeetown...

Llewellyn's probably had a global client list on speed dial.

Pete was the first to peel off from the group and go back to the truck. He pulled out a cooler of pop and carried it to the back porch. He raised the lid and looked at Bernie.

"No thanks, I'm good."

"Okay, you yahoos. Let's get this stuff moved and then you can take a last look before Bernie sells that thing." He glanced over to him again, "You're not thinking about keeping it in this barn, are you? You need an alarm system and more security than that pup!"

Perspicacious man, that Pete. "It's sturdy," Bernie started.

Pete rolled his eyes. "It's a fire trap."

"It's locked. I bought a security light and a camera. Is not a fire trap; it's stood for thirty years!"

"It's almost wet season, so that's in your favor. The more people hear about this car, though, the more likely you are to have trouble."

"Wouldn't the car stand out like a sore thumb? How could someone steal it and get away with it? I haven't tried to start it, but I doubt it runs. I need a good mechanic, by the way."

"There's a guy named Rex at the park. Not sure he's in this league, though. There's a mechanic in town but I doubt he'd let you take it to his shop."

"Why not?"

"Wouldn't insurance be an issue?"

"Oh. That again." Bernie thought about it, "maybe he would come out here as a side job? Or one of his guys? Who are you talking about?"

Pete told him, and then offered to talk to him first.

"As to stealing it, some folks are just plain mean. Vandalism happens. Jealousy? Isn't there some kind of issue about where it came from?" Pete reached over and stroked Puppy's head. "Hey, Doodle."

"Word travels fast," Bernie answered wryly. "I'm going to have to get that title settled sooner than later."

"Doodle? Where did that come from?" Ralph asked as he joined them, he'd heard what Pete called the pup, even if it *had* gone over Bernie's head.

Pete looked a little embarrassed. "Well, Bernie here hasn't told me what he's named him, and Doris and Patty have been referring to him as a "Cocker-doodle-doo" or just 'Doodle.'

JJ joined them. "So does Aunt Catherine."

Bernie looked down at the fluffy, cream-colored pup with hairy feet. "No."

The puppy shrank.

"I'm not yelling at you, good dog." Bernie ruffled his ears, "but 'Doodle' is not a respectable name for a watchdog."

Doodle wagged his tail at hearing what he apparently thought was his name.

CHAPTER 13   FRIDAY

It was a little lighter in the little bedroom that was doing double duty as an office. Still, as dark and gloomy as it was outside, it was still gloomy inside. The storm had passed on, but the clouds lingered. Vicious lay on a rag rug in the middle of the room. 'Vicious' was probably not going to stick. There wasn't a vicious bone in that dog's athletic little body.

"Was there any mention of a vehicle in my uncle's will?" Bernie had his lawyer and his phone on speaker.

"Not specifically. He just left everything to you if he was pre-deceased by his wife."

The family lawyer was tapping his pen on his desk. Bernie could hear it. He'd known him forever and seen him tap it when distracted.

"I found an old car in the barn and am looking for a title so I can sell it." He felt a little guilty at how seriously he was downplaying the find.

"He would probably have it with his home records. There wasn't anything in the will, and I don't believe he had a safe deposit box or anything. Is there a safe in the house? Lots of old houses have a safe built-in somewhere... Maybe behind a picture, or in the floor under a rug? What about his insurance company? Have you talked to them?

"Sorry, I can't be of more help..."

"That's okay, thanks for your time." Now Bernie was tapping *his* pen on the desk. He'd been through all the drawers, even eyeballing them to see if they had false bottoms. He felt vaguely James-Bondian as he did so and thought about what Betty would say regarding the comparison. For the first time in a very long time, he was able to smile when he thought of her.

Still smiling, he headed to the first floor, to start looking behind pictures.

"A safe, huh?" Ralph commented. "Don't suppose his desk is one of those with all the secret compartments and catches."

"Don't I wish."

"Okay, okay. I suppose you've looked behind all the pictures and under the rugs."

Bernie gave him a wry look. "I was in the middle of it when you came in."

Ralph popped the top of one of the beer cans he had brought over. "Sorry to interrupt; I'll take my beer elsewhere!"

"Don't leave. I'm just grouchy. Patches and Rex were chasing around the house a little bit ago and knocked over a lamp."

"Rex?"

"Yeah, I know. He's not really a 'Rex' either, is he? I'm done down here and was about to start upstairs. I'll order pizza if you want to help."

The two men trooped up the stairs with the pup between them, bounding a few steps and then waiting for the slower men to catch up.

Ralph set his beer on the desk and turned his attention to the wall behind the recliner.

The cat, Patches, exploded from underneath it as the pup jumped up on the chair to help. Patches leaped to the desk, caught the blotter with one claw, and yanked it out from under the beer can.

A sheet of paper shifted from under the blotter. The beer-puddle was moving steadily toward it as both men saw and grabbed for the paper.

Bernie was bigger and landed on his brother even as Ralph snatched it away from the slowly flowing beer.

"Hey! Get off, you big lug!"

"Sorry. Is that what I think it is?" Bernie tried to get up without hurting the body under him.

"How am I supposed to know before I can even see it?"

The two sat on the floor and Bernie reached for the paper. Ralph reluctantly handed it over, "I found it and saved it, after all."

"Yeah, but it was your beer." Bernie groused as he looked at the paper. He turned it sideways twice

Ralph turned the can upright and used the hem of his tee shirt to soak up the puddle.

Bernie looked at him in disgust. "Take that off and I'll wash it with mine. Grab another from my room."

"You're bigger than I am, it'll fit like a pup tent."

"You're scrawny, what did Heather ever see in you?"

That hit a nerve. "I'm not scrawny, you're a gorilla." Ralph frowned and Bernie remembered Heather had left him.

"Sorry, Bro." At a loss as to how to fix his insensitive remark, Bernie floundered. "Do your own damn laundry, then. Order a pizza. They have my credit card.

"I may have to call the lawyer back. It looks like one guy signed it over to a man named Harold. Then Harold wrote what I think looks like a bill of sale in the margins signing it over to Uncle Sean against an IOU."

"So, he really did win it in a card game."

"Gambling is unlawful. But, also irrelevant. It doesn't say what the IOU was for. It doesn't really matter.

"Looks like I need to get to town. A title is the first step unless I want to do a "Harold" and write another bill of sale in a different margin. Want to go?"

"What happened to pizza? It'll be here in a few minutes. Oops. I forgot. I'm picking up Tina in a little bit and we're going to the beach for a barbecue with her cousin Michael and some friends of his. I'm cook and we're chaperones."

Bernie burst out laughing. "YOU are a chaperone? I should go just to watch *you*."

"Well, I think we're more like chauffeurs. For some maggoty reason, kids don't get driver's licenses anymore." Then Ralph thought to add, "And YOU are definitely NOT going. Tina was a little put out that I took your place with the plate.

Until I'm sure you're off her horizon..."

Bernie was still grinning on the way to town. Cold pizza was chilling in the 'fridge for dinner...

CHAPTER 14 SATURDAY

Patty came around the corner of the house looking for Bernie. Actually, she was looking for the dog, but she supposed it was more socially acceptable to be looking for the man of the house, first.

"Hey! Bernie!"

"Back here!"

Patty picked her way carefully through the thigh-high weeds between the house and the barn. She was going to have grass seed *EVERYWHERE.* "You need a weed-whacker?" She grumbled under her breath.

The puppy came bounding toward her.

Bernie heard her.

"Got one. I need more time to use it." Bernie clapped his hands, "Zeus! Down!"

The puppy looked back out of caution but sidled up to Patty anyway.

Patty just laughed. "Zeus? You have to be kidding. Does he really answer to that?" She reached down to ruffle his ears, "Good boy…"

"Do NOT call him that name!" Bernie roared.

Both Patty and the dog raised their eyebrows at his temerity.

"Excuse me?" Patty asked, frostily.

"I will not have my respectable watchdog going by that undignified name!"

"Well, I hate to tell you this, but he's certainly not a Zeus."

"Maybe not. I'll keep trying. Suggestions are welcome," he offered, to take the sting out of the last couple of minutes.

"Okay, I'll think on it. Meanwhile, I brought him some treats. I used to make and sell my own dog food and treats – Buddy was allergic to corn. In those days it was hard to get dog food without it, not like today. So, I had to make it for him." She absently stroked Doodle's ears. "My treats were always popular with all the dogs, though. These are peanut butter and yam." She started to hand him a plastic bag,

"You're busy, I'll just hang these on your back door."

"What are you working on?" She called back to him as she went up his back steps.

"Come see."

"I'm shorter than you, if I disappear in your landscaping, call 911."

Bernie gave a snort and led the way to the back corner of the barn. "I'm pulling weeds out of the raspberry bushes. At least, I think that's what they are."

There was a neat rectangle of what passed for dirt in Florida. Just beyond one corner was a scraggly patch half cleared out of grass and weeds. Patty pulled out her phone, and using an app, pointed her camera at some of the leaves. "Yup. Raspberries. Says they need fertilizer."

"Let me see that." He reached for her phone. "This is pretty neat."

She took her phone back. "I'll text you a link. How far did you get yesterday trying to get a new title?"

Bernie made a face. "If I'd thought it through, I could have saved myself a few hours. As it is, I have to go back on Monday with a copy of the will and Uncle Sean's death certificate."

"I'm surprised they didn't want that other guy to come in with you."

"Harold? They did ask. He's dead, too." "You want some tea or something? I was about to take a break."

"No, you weren't. I gotta go, anyway." She turned around, "Bye, Doo..." She hesitated and looked at Bernie.

He suggested, "King?" Then he grinned as she laughed all the way around the corner of the house.

He had set up the repaired bee boxes in another corner of the garden and was somewhat patiently scooping bird seed out of a 40-pound bag with a heavy trowel, then pouring it into the ridiculously small opening at the top of a bird feeder. There had to be a better way of doing it. A funnel? If he had three hands…

Two more birdfeeders to go.

He came around the corner of the house to the feeder he had hung near the front window. A woman about his age was climbing out of a muddy yellow rust bucket. Zeus headed for her. "Stop, Zeus. Sit."

Zeus sat.

Surprise!

"Are you Bernie?"

"I am. You are?" Bernie set the bag down heavily to flatten the bottom so it wouldn't tip over.

Should he reach out to shake hands? Who was she and why did she look mad?

"Caroleen Hemmings."

The last name was familiar. It had been scrawled on the back of the title to the car. "You must be Harold's widow?"

"I am. More importantly, I'm the

owner of that car you found, and I want it back, now."

Zeus didn't like her tone and came to sit at Bernie's feet.

Somehow, Bernie hadn't anticipated meeting this woman. Maybe at one of the carshows in the future; after the car was history, so to speak.

"I'm sorry. Your husband signed the title over to my Uncle Sean. I took the title to the DMV yesterday and it is being re-titled to me." Just a little exaggeration, there. 'They' had assured him that with the proper documentation, there would be no problem – and he was going back the day after tomorrow.

While he was talking to her, he took in small details. Her salmon-colored hair hadn't been brushed or combed. There were stains on her orange day dress. Her gray tennis shoes had a hole in one toe. The bag of birdseed probably outweighed her.

"Liar! I know what that car is worth!

My Harold would never have given it up! He knew how much I loved that car!"

Zeus stood up and bristled. Bernie automatically reached down to smooth his fur and calm him down. "Good dog."

To the woman, though, he was less comforting. "Oh, give it a rest! I looked at the dates on the back of the title. You two only owned it for about six weeks, and he never even bothered to get it re-titled. You're just mad because he lost it gambling and you've worked up a thirty-year mad. Go home and forget about it." He took a step towards her without even realizing he was doing it.

"I'll be back with the law!" She turned and retreated fearfully. "Chase an old woman, will you?!"

"You're no older than I am!" The accusation that he was a bully stung him. He could practically see Mama rolling over in her grave.

Bernie fumed as he finished filling the feeders, scattering seed in all directions, and then poured the diminished bag of seed into his new can just inside the barn. He was going to have to move it. If he got in the habit of putting everything just inside the door to the barn, he would have a mess again in no time.

Later.

He pulled the door to, behind him. He turned back and secured the lock. No point in a lock if he didn't use it. He gave it a tug for good measure.

"Want to go to town with me, Champ?"

"Woof!"

CHAPTER 15   WEDNESDAY

"I'll have to admit, I'm a little wary of

playing cards at your house." Patty gave a furtive look past his back porch toward the big Live Oak in his yard.

"Why?"

"Have you seen the Leprechaun since that night?"

"What leprechaun?"

"Oh, come on, Bernie; be serious!"

"I am serious. You're an adult. Have you ever seen one before? I think we were victims of mass hysteria or something. You can go back there and look. I have." Bernie asserted.

"You stubborn Irishman. You're more Irish than I am, and *I* don't doubt the wee folk!"

"We're here!" Ralph called cheerfully from the front door. Catherine was laboriously using her walker to get up the steps while Ralph held the door for her.

"I like it." Dr Catherine asserted as she stood in the middle of the parlor.

"Show me the rest." They went back to the hallway, and she amended the request, "The first floor, anyway. Those stairs don't look mobility-issue-friendly. Especially with a rambunctious puppy. "What's his name today?"

"Champ." Bernie stated firmly.

"Well, that's the best one so far..." Ralph nodded.

They settled, finally, at the drop-leaf table in the dining room.

"I'm thinking about taking that wall out, or at least making a pass-through to the kitchen."

"Great! I have a sledgehammer!" Ralph volunteered.

"How *did* you grow to adulthood with all those violent tendencies? Why didn't someone beat you and feed you to an alligator?" Catherine asked.

"It's his endearing enthusiasm. It outweighs his dangerous quirks." Bernie carried a plate stacked with blueberry turnovers and four bowls. "Dessert first!" He set down a can of whipped cream. "Don't say it, Patty. I'm a bachelor, I'm allowed short-cut whipped cream!"

Patty closed her mouth.

"That was great, Big Brother! Now tell us about the latest on the car." Ralph stopped shuffling and started dealing.

Sometime later, Bernie and Patty were winning, so Ralph decided it was time for distraction. "Pete says his mechanic's business insurance doesn't cover people's cars; they're covered by their own providers. So, he'll be happy to tow it in if you can't start it, and take a look at what it needs. Also, he won't come to the house. Rex will, but…"

Patty gave an indelicate snort at the mention of the anarchist who lived in their mobile home park.

"I talked to a couple of insurance

companies." Bernie discarded and Dr. Catherine picked it up.

"Cars or cards, boys. You're men and you can't concentrate on both at once," declared Patty.

They ignored her.

"There are only a couple who will even talk about it. They talked to the tune of about $5000 a year."

Ralph discarded to Patty, and she picked it up.

"Never mind, Ralph, talk all you want;" Patty changed gears.

Patches wandered through and Bernie put his bowl on the floor so she could finish the little bits of whipped cream. He looked sideways at his Cocker-Doodle. "Champ" was much more tolerant of Patches than vice-versa and was ignoring her.

Thunder shook the very framework of the old house. There was a loud cracking sound outside followed by a muffled crash.

Bernie dropped his cards on the table and rose to go see.

"Wait. I'll go with you." Ralph was on his heels as they dashed out the back door to the narrow porch.

Champ peered into the darkness looming over the already wet grass and had zero interest in leaving the porch. He barked just to show he was on the job, however.

Another bolt of lightning illuminated the yard.

Lightning had hit a large oak tree and one side had split off from halfway up. The fall was softened by the hundreds of smaller branches, twigs and leaves as literally half of a hundred-year-old tree fell in front of the door to the barn.

The tree hadn't hit the roof, just made an impenetrable green wall between the house and the barn. It looked to be more nuisance than a problem.

The sky opened up and there was a

roar as rain pounded down on the metal roof.

"You guys might as well stay until the rain stops. Whose turn was it?" Bernie led the way back in.

"That could be all night. The end of this hand, then we have to be getting back," Dr Catherine answered.

CHAPTER 16   THURSDAY

It was damned hard to see, but dark

was best. This blasted tree was a blessing in some ways.

She just wanted to see it.

Okay, she just wanted it back, now that the grapevine had told her it was here, in a freaking barn no less!

It had never occurred to her that the car was still here, this close by. If that old coot, Sean, could hide it practically in plain sight, she could do the same and keep it in her garage until no one cared!

Her companion got tired of stepping over and around, he grabbed a branch and snapped it off, tossing it aside.

"Quiet, you idiot. The car will make noise when you start it, and then we'll have to hurry. We don't want anyone coming out now."

The grunt from her companion was only what she expected, so she tried again to pry the hasp loose from the wood. "This tree is hiding us from the house, but you'll have to drive around it when we get the door open. Why don't you go check out a path to get out?"

"It's dark out here. What if that dog comes out? And I've heard there are bears back here."

"So, grab a stick, you ninny. And keep your voice down! I'm not giving you the knife – I'm using it."

She'd gotten the tip under a screw head and was getting encouraged when she heard him come back. She looked over her shoulder and saw him out of the corner of her eye. She saw a glint as he tossed a bottle away. She turned back to her task. "I can tell you've been drinking. You never have had a lick of sense, coming out here soused," she hissed viciously. "Back off, you smell like a wet dog," she growled at him and looked back to glare at him. He'd always been intimidated by her scowls. She saw a movement behind him.

Her brother had no idea they weren't alone. He whined, "Yeah, well, you couldn't do this without me, could you?"

The dark figure loomed behind him as Caroleen glanced back. She jumped up, hitting his chin with her head and swiped blindly with her knife.

Her brother let out a roar as he jerked away from her. "I knew I couldn't trust you!" He swung the broken branch. It connected with a soft thud. He dropped the stick she'd *told* him to find and ran.

The figure from behind him stood and looked down at the woman on the ground, picked up the bottle, then lumbered off into the darkness.

The cardinals and the woodpeckers were discussing the weather when Bernie went out to face storm damage. Funny how noisy it always was at this time of day.

He'd eaten breakfast – eggs, sausage, and biscuits, and strawberries, telling himself he would need the calories for the upcoming yard work. Then he had a second cup of coffee, for planning purposes. No need to go off half-cocked. One advantage to living alone was that you could start whatever big project you had, anytime you wanted. It didn't *have* to be the butt-crack of dawn.

It felt disloyal to complain about one of Betty's more lamentable traits when she wasn't there to defend herself.

But breakfast had been good! It was still *reasonably* early.

He fetched a rope from his truck and started pulling on smaller branches. Twigs grabbed and snagged at his shirt. He cussed under his breath as he broke his way to the middle. He needed to clear a way to attach the rope to the split trunk. Then he could use the truck to pull everything away from the barn door. Then he could get to his tools and cut it up properly.

He pulled the rope taut and dragged, tearing the base of the enormous tree, splitting farther down the tree until it gave way and he had to slam on his brakes before his momentum carried him right onto his porch. After a deep breath, he looked back, and he saw a bright slash on the ground near the front of the barn.

When he had recovered from his astonishment and was sure the woman was beyond any rudimentary first aid he might be able to offer, he fetched his phone from inside to call 911. While on the phone, he noticed a depression in the garden, about 20 inches long and nearly a foot wide, between her and the woods. Another similar depression was just at the edge of the grass, half in the sandy garden. There may have been more, closer, but dragging the tree had effectively erased any other marks in the sand. It had also played havoc with his fire pit.

While he was on the phone, the rain started again and had already collapsed the edges and filled in the bottoms of the depressions. They were gone – no chance to photograph or measure!

The Detective from the Sheriff's Office, Dan, had his notebook out and was writing. Water was dripping off the branches over their heads. Dan stepped back too late and water spilled onto his notebook. He had to start a new page. Then, he had stepped back right into the cleared space of the garden patch, sinking unevenly into the soft ground.

There was nothing there to disturb at the moment, but that was where the depressions had been, Bernie thought ruefully.

"I understand you two had met?" Dan inquired mildly.

Bernie examined Dan's face for sarcasm but didn't find any in the man's expression.

"You could say that." Bernie went on to explain, in the same vein of understatement Dan had begun. "She was – unpleasant."

"I heard you chased her across your yard with a machete."

Bernie's surprise was evident.

Dan nodded, "yeah, I thought so. No witnesses, though; that makes it 'she-said-he-said,' and she was certifiable."

"How did you know she was even here?" Bernie asked curiously.

"She called my wife to make an official complaint."

"Does your wife work for the Sheriff's Office, too?"

"No. Which is one reason I hadn't bothered you about it yet. Another reason was that she was on your property, apparently uninvited. Plus, if I know her at all, which I do, she was probably threatening *you.*" Dan sighed, though. "Still... I know I was busy; but if I'd come out sooner, maybe she wouldn't have felt it necessary to come out here again on her own."

"Maybe I should have called in; I had been told she was, well, unstable." Bernie felt the need to lift a little of the guilt off the detective's shoulders.

The medical examiner arrived and shooed them away. The rain had stopped but started again. They moved under the canopy of a palm tree and Dan turned a page in his notebook.

"Did you touch the body?"

"Just to see if there was a pulse."

"Tell me again how you found her."

Bernie walked him through his clean-up effort. He mentioned the huge print in the garden bed. "I don't remember bears being that large, here." He tentatively gave the detective an opening to discuss alternative wildlife in the area. He was reluctant to throw out the cryptid theory and move himself into the deputy's 'certifiable' category.

Dan arched an eyebrow. "They're not. Maybe it was just a scrape from the branch dragging over it."

It was apparent the detective was not interested in, nor impressed with the possible prints.

"What time did the tree fall? Were you up or did it wake you up?"

"We were playing cards when lightning hit the tree about ten or so last night."

"Who is 'we?'"

"Ralph, Dr Catherine, Patty and I."

Dan ran his hand over his face and groaned. Patty had been involved in every unexplained death in the area in the past couple of years. Of course, there hadn't *been* any unexplained deaths until she moved there.

In a way, it had been easier to investigate these things before he had become friends with her (and co-parents to a flock of chickens and a duck, but that was another story.) To be fair, though, she was smart and had been frequently (and recklessly) a big help.

Dan couldn't help but look sideways at this other newcomer, though, as well. This was the second body associated with

Bernie. What *was* the county coming to?

"Please tell me they went home without anyone coming out here."

"They went home without anyone coming out here."

"Truly?"

Bernie laughed. "Yeah. It was raining so we didn't venture out. They left after we finished that hand, though."

"All of them? You saw them all leave?"

"You sound surprised and suspicious – why?"

"Miss Patty just always seems to be in the middle of things."

Bernie thought back to the Leprechaun, and laughed, "I'd heard that about her." Suddenly he felt guilty about laughing only yards from the unfortunate woman on the ground.

"I don't know what Ms. Hemmings thought she was going to do out here in the middle of the night in a storm. There was a knife on the ground by her. She may have been planning some vandalism, but that doesn't make sense when the last I heard, she loved the car. Have you actually started it? Does it run? Maybe she was going to lure you out and hurt you? I'm not a mechanic, but even I know the chances of it starting and going very far seem fairly remote."

Bernie nodded. "Curiosity sounds possible, but she struck me as more of in revenge mode. I'll bet more on thinking she *could* steal it. Is she a mechanic, though? Now, when she couldn't start it, *then* I could see vandalism. She was certainly nasty enough when she was here a couple of days ago. No, by the way, I haven't started it yet; I'm not sure about the fuel in the system."

"The barn has a new lock on it." Dan noticed.

"I was waiting for the title and registration to put insurance on the car. I *did* figure it had been safe in there for thirty years... but better safe than sorry."

"Yes, it was safe, because no one knew it was in there. General consensus was that he drove it north. Now *everyone* knows it's here."

"Insurance is in the works. Finding someone to insure it was an unexpected hassle."

"We should all have those problems." Dan tucked his little notebook into his pocket and brought the conversation back to the unfortunate woman. "Please wait here, I need to speak to the M. E. about a few things."

CHAPTER 17 *STILL* THURSDAY

Later, at his house, Ralph just shook his head. "We should have gone out there. We might have been able to help her, then."

"Completely discounting the fact that she was violent, trespassing, deranged, and had a knife..." Bernie commented wryly.

"Well, yes. I suppose that suggestion may have seemed disloyal."

"Or else it makes me sound like a bastard for not caring..." Bernie added.

"No one who knows you would think that. You're a big Teddy Bear."

"Thank you; I thought I was intimidating. Now you impugn my manhood."

Bernie was still perseverating about the woman. "We're assuming the falling tree hit her and killed her. There were large, er, possible tracks nearby. Maybe a scavenger, but maybe a predator? What am I missing here that no one wants to talk about? An escaped gorilla from the wildlife park?"

"You won't find any non-native species in any of the state parks – against the rules. Well, except one hippopotamus. They don't even have parrots anymore. Gorillas are definitely non-native – unless you count Tina's brother."

"That's right! How did the beach thing go?"

Ralph waggled his eyebrows. "Wouldn't you like to know! Honestly, the kids were great. We only had to chase one couple back to the sand after they'd disappeared into the woods around the boardwalk and pier.

"Her uncle is something else. Kind of a throwback to the last century. Tina's dad moved into her house after her husband died. So, she was taking care of him. Then her dad died, and her uncle moved in 'to take care of' her." Ralph was using air quotes. "*His* wife had died in 'an unfortunate accident' a few months earlier. He's more of a burden than a guardian, though; a ne'er-do-well if I've ever met one. Those air quotes were hers. Tina is more of a mom to the boy than a cousin. I guess there's another sister to Tina's uncle and dad, but they don't talk about her. Carl's teenager, Michael, referred to her once as the crazy aunt."

"Enough gossip." Ralph wanted to change topics again. "Did you take pictures of the tracks? We might find someone who can identify them."

"No, they kind of melted back into the sand while I was calling 911."

"Tough luck. Can you draw them?" Ralph asked, hopefully, and fetched him paper and a pen from his junk drawer.

Ralph studied the somewhat amorphous shape Bernie produced. "What makes you think that's any kind of track?"

Doubt crept back into Bernie's mind. If even his brother was skeptical – and *he* tended to believe anything Bernie told him... not saying his brother was gullible or anything...

"I guess I got the idea from the U-Pick Berry Place the other day. The one across the woods from my place. Something had damaged some of their plants.

"The bakery-lady, Hattie, seemed to think there might be something bigger than 'possums, or even bears, in the wetland area, there."

"Could be a Swamp Ape!" Ralph used 'air quotes' to take any serious consideration away from his response.

Bernie rolled his eyes impatiently. *Where HAD Ralph picked up that annoying air-quote habit?*

"I'm taking Tina out tonight. I'll ask her if she's seen anyone or 'anything' lurking around." Ralph leered.

"Hattie, huh? Huh?"

"Come on, Ralph, we just had coffee."

Dan reflexively pet the duck, Moe, as he asked Patty again, "What happened after you saw the tree was down?"

She sipped her root beer Kool-Aid and eyed her friend over the edge of her pickle jar tumbler. "Why do I get the impression this is no longer just a curious accident that happened to a trespasser with nefarious intent?"

"Do I have to get out my notebook and make this official?" Dan complained.

"Oh, I suppose I can cooperate. After the lightning struck and the tree fell, we all ran to the back porch. Well, all of us but Catherine. Mobility issues just suck." she editorialized.

"I was stuck in the doorway because the guys got there first. So, I had a little higher vantage point. The light from the house showed the tree was down. We couldn't see clearly, of course, it was dark. Another bolt of lightning lit up the sky briefly and we could see how big a piece of the tree had fallen. Then it resumed pouring buckets, so we went back inside.

"Bernie offered for us to stay late or stay the night, but that's just because he lived away so long. Nobody here cares about a little rain."

Patty stopped, and Dan had to prompt her to get her going again. "So..."

"Oh! Well, we finished that hand and Catherine said it was time for us to go. Ralph had taken us in his truck, so we all left together."

"What time did you get home?"

"About eleven or so." Patty frowned, "maybe a little later. Not much, though." She was stroking the mottled feathers of Eanie. "So, what's up?"

Dan laughed and put their adopted duck back in the run on her porch. "You know better than that. Don't leave town!" He winked at her; at least this time she wasn't a suspect!

"About eleven-thirty," Ralph

estimated.

"Eleven-fifteen, sharp," answered Catherine confidently.

"Didn't believe me?" Patty called across the small patch of grass separating her little camper from Catherine's Taj Majal of Trailers. Dan just waved at her as he got back into his vehicle.

Dan found himself back at Bernie's house before noon. "What time did you go to bed last night?"

"Hmm. Must have been about eleven-thirty."

"You're not sure? Was it still raining?"

"Don't know. Oh, yes. I mean yes, I do know. No, it wasn't it had stopped. Killer, here, went out to do his business. He's kind of a sissy about getting wet, so it must have stopped, at least for a bit."

"Killer?" Dan asked, mildly.

"We're looking for a suitable name. I

admit that one might be a little macabre, considering, but I'm trying to keep everyone from calling him D-o-o-d-l-e."

Bernie spelled it to keep his dog from hearing it.

"So, not long after your friends left, you went to bed. Did you go right to sleep?"

"Pretty much. I learned in the service to sleep when I could – it never takes me long to turn off and drop off."

"Viet Nam?"

"Yeah."

"Did you wake up at all after that?"

"Not until morning. Patches gets me up every morning."

Daniel looked around.

"You won't see her. She's been scarce since Doo... Killer came."

"What did you do after you got up?"

Bernie went through his breakfast, again. "I've already told you all this."

"Never hurts to hear it again, you might remember seeing or hearing something else. No noise or commotion outside? Maybe when Doo… The killer went out in the morning?"

Bernie swallowed a sharp retort. "No. This is starting to sound like a murder investigation." Bernie was losing patience with what he considered to be a cut-and-dried accident. He sighed. He had to admit, if only to himself if it *hadn't* been an accident, he certainly had an excellent motive for doing in the old bat. "Don't you have anything better to do?"

Dan continued patiently. "What time did you go out to start removing the tree?"

"Subtract maybe a half-hour from my 911 call. I don't wear a watch – who does, anymore? The only clock is on the microwave in the kitchen or on my phone. I didn't look, because I didn't care."

Bernie had just about had enough.

He was a patient man but finding the dead woman in his yard had just about used up his equanimity. "Can I finish cleaning up the tree back there? The deputies told me I had to stay out of the backyard until they were done. Can't see what's taking so long when she was clearly hit by the tree."

"To be clear, you did not leave the house between going to bed and when you went out to move the tree."

"No. I did not."

"Thank you. If you think of anything else, call me. You're not planning on going anywhere, are you?"

"Only the landfill, if I can ever finish cutting that up," Bernie replied testily. "I'm not leaving town if that's what you're asking me."

CHAPTER 18   FRIDAY

"There were indications that *her* fall, and subsequent death, occurred sometime *after* the tree fell," the medical examiner informed the detective.

"The head wound was not from the bloody tree branch?" Dan was incredulous.

"Oh, yes. It was definitely a match to the wound. You'll remember it was not on top of the body, however. And the trajectory of the blow seems to indicate a more horizontal blow."

"If she had been bending down, head to one side... It was obvious from the marks on the door she was trying to jimmy the lock." Dan closed his eyes to picture it better. "As to where the branch was found,

Mr. Murphy had dragged everything awry."

"Your job to figure that out, not mine," decried the M. E., "I just offer the facts. The ground was wet underneath her, and there were no scratches or cuts on the part of her body facing up towards the remaining tree," the man said defensively, "except, of course, the head wound. Her clothes were not soaked through as if she'd been there through the storm; more like just from the dew."

"The tree did not fall on top of her." Now that he had surprised the detective and defended his findings, he needed to admit a failing. "There was a minuscule bit of I thought would be blood on the knife blade," the medical examiner hesitated, "completely unidentifiable."

"What do you mean by 'unidentifiable'?" Dan demanded.

Defensive again, the M.E. snapped back. "Exactly what I said. It very diluted and might not be blood, but that is as close as I can come. It doesn't match anything else, much less *anyone*."

He retreated to scientific terms to regain his professional respect. "The precipitin test showed the possible blood was not human."

When in professional doubt, deflect, "Look up cryptids."

Big Foot and the Bentley

CHAPTER 19   SATURDAY

Dan got out of his vehicle again a couple of hours later. He wished he had another suspect besides Bernie Murphy, but he did not. He'd been going over Caroleen's file – not surprising that she had one – and trying to contact anyone she had ever fought with. Her most serious altercations had been with her late husband (dead-end, pun intended) and her brother. He was still looking for the brother, Carl. He didn't own property, pay taxes, or have a bank account or a car.

Bernie was in the front yard laying bricks around a tree. He stood slowly as the little cream-colored dog with big hairy feet, Killer, ran up to Dan and thrust his nose into his hand to get petted.

"Back so soon?" Bernie asked tried not to sound sarcastic.

The detective reached down to pet the little dog and raised his eyebrows in mute query.

"Still Killer."

Dan couldn't help it, he laughed.

"About my visit, though," he gave a small smile. "Sometimes things aren't as clear as they could be. I've come back to look at the barn again. Come with me?

"Tell me again about what you saw on the ground." Dan was examining the knife marks on the wood around the new lock and hardware on the front barn door, again. He knew he was on shaky ground asking about the tracks, but there had been other reports of a large hominid, for lack of a better description, in the area.

His personal opinion or not, he needed to follow up.

"Our parents would have called it a gruagach. That's the Irish name for the Big

Foot," Bernie clarified. "Ralph laughed at me and said they were Florida Big Foot tracks. I think we called them Swamp Apes when we were kids, but I had forgotten about them until Ralph brought them up.

Testily, Dan persisted. "I want to hear *you* describe them again. I can talk to Ralph, later."

"Did I hear my name?" Ralph came up behind them.

"I was just telling the detective, here, about the tracks I saw. I'm not sure if he's taking me seriously, or not." Bernie looked sideways at the deputy. "Ralph was going to ask Tina if she'd seen anyone or any big animals around."

He looked at Dan, "Tina lives just up the road and has taken a shine to my little brother, here."

"Sorry, Bro. When I went to get her for our date yesterday, she said she'd had a death in the family and burst into tears. Her uncle was home and yelling in the background.

"Tina said she couldn't leave him or Michael alone and I'd better leave. She didn't have to tell me twice. He's a mean one when he's sober! I'd hate to tangle with him when he's drunk."

Dan looked startled. "What's the uncle's name?"

"Carl," Ralph answered.

"Thank you, Gentlemen." Dan hurried off.

Bernie scratched his head. "Are Tina and the boy safe with the guy?"

"Tina is too smart to let him get close enough to hurt her. The boy has grown up dodging him." Ralph headed to Bernie's refrigerator after a bottle – all this talk about beer was making him thirsty. "Actually, Michael is at least as big as his father. Not as muscular, just big." He handed a bottle to Bernie.

"Thank goodness for small favors that Michael doesn't take after Carl. He's smart enough that his size and IQ would make him a formidable criminal. But, he's kind of a loner. Tina says she barely sees him unless he's hungry."

Doodle begged for a treat and Bernie got one of Patty's out of the cookie jar.

Ralph looked a little green. "Dog treats in your cookie jar?"

Bernie laughed. "Don't worry. Patty says they won't hurt you."

Dan was frankly trying to get a rise out of the man across the interview table. He slumped, trying to look unconcerned. He reeked of alcohol, cigarettes, and too infrequent showers.

"Where were you Wednesday night?"

"At home; asleep."

"I talked to your boss. You got off about six and walked across the street to join a woman."

"I don't work." Carl shifted his gaze to the door.

"Your boss concurs."

"I can't work." He rubbed his hands through his stubble. "Pain, you know."

"I understand you're not an employee. I'm not from the IRS. However, he does pay you to fix cars sometimes, and he said you were there Wednesday afternoon. When you left, where did you go?"

"I ate dinner with my sister. Is that a crime?"

"You still have a restraining order against her, even though you have apparently moved from your last known address."

"I can move. I take care of my niece."

"Mm-hmmm. Where did you go after dinner?"

"Home."

"Where did your sister go?"

"How the hell should I know?"

"You didn't talk to her again?"

"No. When Tina woke me up Thursday evening, she told me a tree fell on Caroleen."

"Why did you sleep all day Thursday instead of showing up at your" Dan cleared his throat "*friend's* shop to work on cars?"

"I didn't sleep good. Pain, you know."

"So you said. Where was your boy all this time?"

"School."

"You sure about that? Does he ever see his aunt?"

Dan just wanted to see if he could catch a flicker of worry or doubt. About his job, his niece, his boy... "I'm pulling your phone records."

Carl thought about it after he got home. *Stupid cop. He'd been lying to law enforcement since he was eight; no way was one going to catch him out now.*

He took a long pull off his beer and thought about the dispatcher. Thinking about the dispatcher put him in a better mood – the woman in a uniform thing, you know.

Handcuffs.

Then he thought some more about his sister and the car. There were no calls or messages between him and Caroleen. She didn't hold with technology like cell phones and didn't even have one.

He hadn't seen or heard from her since the pandemic started.

For some reason, Caroleen had blamed him for the death of his wife.

Like he could have expected his wife to fling herself out of the truck like that while he was driving down the highway? He'd nearly wrecked his vehicle!

Caroleen was *his* sister, not *hers*. But, Caroleen had tried to shoot him after that.

The sheriff took her guns away and he'd had to file a restraining order. Then he hadn't seen her or talked to her in years.

Until she turned up out of the blue, wanting his help.

He almost hadn't recognized her. She'd gotten old and slovenly. She had been an odd duck all her life.

She was still an odd duck, right up until she'd taken a swipe at him with her knife that night.

He still didn't understand that. But the more he thought about it, he was pretty sure his swing was self-defense.

Considering the circumstances of where they were and what they were doing, though, keeping his mouth shut was best. It wasn't as if there was any other family to care.

Suddenly Carl sat bolt upright as another thought hit him.

He had a house of his own, now. He was her closest relative! He and Michael should move in before anyone else questioned it.

Don't they say possession is 9/10ths of the law?

She had a car, too.

He was pretty sure that detective had the car, though.

He picked up his phone. Now, who had a truck and could help him move his stuff?

As the phone began to ring a drinking buddy's number, he bellowed "Michael! Where the hell are you? Get packed, we're moving!"

CHAPTER 20   MONDAY

Dan was just a hair disgruntled. He wasn't sure who it was who had seen the pages he had printed out regarding Big Foot. He should never have printed them. But it was just like his notebook, he liked the feel of paper and the ability to make notes in the margins.

It had been an idle search on his part when he'd reached an impasse with Carl. First, the M.E. had thrown out completely off-the-wall forensic information. Then Bernie – a no-nonsense, reliable man if he'd ever met one – had brought up Big Foot. Lastly, there had been Ralph's input on footprints. What was the county coming to?

Now he was stuck with the fall-out. Someone had heard he'd been researching "cryptids," looked them up (he'd had to) and called it in to the paper.

He could just hear the chuckles as the editor included the call in the local opinions page.

He tapped his pen on the desk. He wasn't getting anything done just sitting here.

He wasn't nervous about going out on the street; not really. Lots of people secretly believed in unidentified hominids.

He wasn't idle, either.

He was planning, that's all.

He harrumphed at no one in particular and headed off to see Patty. He would stop and get some grubs for their foster flock.

"Swamp Ape, huh?" Patty met him at

the door to her camper with an unrepentant grin.

Dan had decided the best defense was deflection. "Nothing to do with the current case. It was just a side issue brought up by a couple of people at the same time.

"Some officers do not respect the sanctity of the office printer." He settled into her chair and handed her the bag of grubs.

"Scuttlebutt says her brother." She pulled out a pet chicken – Eenie - and handed it to Dan. "Scuttlebutt also says her brother *is* a Swamp Ape."

"So far, I can't prove he or his phone was there or that he even knew about the car. I don't think anyone wants to admit he told Carl and have Carl focused on him."

"He and Caroleen ate dinner together – for the first time in eons - Wednesday. Everyone in town knows that." Patty shook out some grubs and Eenie visibly weighed being pet overeating treats. Treats won out and Dan dropped her gently back in the run.

"Don't suppose anyone heard any of the conversation," Patty asked.

"No."

CHAPTER 21 TUESDAY

Michael was not exactly pleased with this newest plan. As usual, his dad had not put enough thought into this.

He surveyed the second bedroom in Caroleen's tiny house. It was on a tiny lot in a closely spaced neighborhood of starter – or snowbird – or retiree-on-a-tight-budget homes. The door had been unlocked – that was a surprise until he realized Caroleen had probably not been past the front door in two years and was just out of the habit.

Tightly double-bagged sacks of trash had completely filled this room and the back patio. Now the yard was full. If they didn't get it to the landfill, animals would scatter it all over central Florida. His dad said he was going to put out three cans every week until they were gone.

When Michael was twenty-three, they should be gone.

The kitchen had like a million cans of soup and a microwave. The refrigerator was unplugged. The first thing his dad did was plug it in and deposit all the beer he had brought from Tina's house.

There was no internet. There was basic cable, at least, and a landline.

Seriously, who had landlines anymore?

He strongly suspected his father thought he was going to do the cooking. His dad would probably put the soup can in the microwave and burn the house down.

He thought about how to convince

his father to hook up to the internet.

He suspected his father would take over Caroleen's car, license or no.

So, how was he going to get to school? He'd have to get a job and a car – and a license. Or change schools. He was old enough to drop out, but he had college in his sights. While he inherited his old man's physique, at least he had his mom's brains.

Damn, life gets complicated.

Maybe Tina would let *just him* move back. His dad could stay here all by himself. He grabbed his laptop and headed for the coffee shop he could see from the backyard. He would video call her.

He should never have let this get so far out of hand. How do you squeal on your old man, though?

"No. You're not going to go back to Tina's."

"I'm not staying here with no transportation. What about school?"

"I'll have Caroleen's car when the cops give it back. I'll take you."

"Right..." Michael eyed his father. "If they find your fingerprints in it, you'll be in trouble."

"We walked through the woods."

Michael smiled as his father suddenly realized what he had just admitted to. Carl let out a roar and propelled himself out of the chair.

"I *am* going back to Tina's," Michael shouted as he disappeared out the back door and over the fence.

He had the leverage he wanted – his dad couldn't make him do anything anymore.

CHAPTER 22   WEDNESDAY

Ralph had made spaghetti, deviled eggs, and garlic bread. When Bernie showed up before the others, he had to joke, "I'm coming the farthest and I'm still here first."

"Here comes Patty." All-star's ears went on alert when he heard Patty's voice.

With a quick look for permission, he charged around the neighbor's trailer to hop excitedly around his friend.

She laughed and pulled a treat out of her pocket for him. "What's your name today?" She looked up at Bernie.

"All-star."

"That's a stupid name."

"I know. I'm running out of sensible and manly options. It's better than Halfback."

"No, it's not," declared Patty.

"Sorry, Bro. I gotta agree with Patty, there."

Dr. Catherine was practically in Patty's footsteps as she came up to the table on the carport patio. "I brought dessert."

"Please tell me it's not blueberry anything – I'm blueberried out," complained Patty.

"No; I finally ran out of blueberries."

Catherine smiled at Ralph conspiratorially.

"She gave me the last of them in a smoothie when I stopped by yesterday," Ralph shared, sticking out his tongue and making a face.

Catherine frowned at him.

"Actually, it was good. It was just the idea of 'healthy,' you know?" Ralph clarified quickly lest Dr. Catherine refuse to ever fix him a snack again.

"Rooster," declared Patty. "Who was that cartoon rooster when we were kids? That's a name for a boy — even if it is a dog."

"I am not naming my watchdog after a bully fowl."

"Watchdog? I've been thinking about that..." Ralph finished his last bite of spaghetti with a slurp.

Catherine eyed him with mingled disgust and amusement as she scooped the last of her carefully cut-down-to-an-inch noodles.

"You did get the title paperwork started, right?" The unrepentant slurper asked.

"Yes. Even paid the first insurance premium. Turns out there's another company here in the States that's not quite as expensive as the one in the UK.

"It was still painful, though. As soon as it's operable, it's for sale."

"Can we get to work on your tree, yet?"

"You sure are a glutton for work."

"I'll need your help one of these days," assured Ralph. "Meanwhile, I'm bored and that means I get into trouble around here."

"Please let him work for you..." begged Patty.

"If you think we can clear the tree out in one day, I'll get the car towed to the shop on Friday."

"It'll cost you dinner and beer."

Dan was frowning at Tina.

She was discomfited. This was not an expression she was accustomed to seeing on men's faces. *Well, except for Carl's, maybe. He didn't count as a man as far as she was concerned.*

"What do you mean, gone? Where did he go to?" Dan demanded.

Tina was strangely reluctant to give up her nearest relative. Why was that, she wondered. Besides, Michael was once again upstairs – she'd picked him up and collected his stuff just this morning. The cop hadn't asked about Michael. It was better to end this quickly before he thought to ask about her cousin.

She shrugged and the strap of her dress fell down her arm to her elbow.

She slowly pulled it back to where it belonged, instinctively dragging it out so she could think. Feminine distraction was second nature to her.

He watched the little drama unfold with irritation. He had *NOT* expected to find his favorite suspect not where he'd left him and was not in the mood to appreciate it.

"He moved out yesterday." Tina shared again, just as Michael came down the stairs.

Michael saw the detective and ducked down the hallway toward the rear of the house just as Tina stepped in front of Dan to give her cousin a head start.

"Carl's probably at Caroleen's house," Tina blurted out, trying to further distract him after he deftly side-stepped around her.

It was too late; Dan was halfway down the hallway. There was just something about someone running that made you run after them.

Tina scrambled after and stood in the doorway as Dan clambered over the fence Michael had jumped. Michael was already in the forest.

Dan's face was a thundercloud as he abandoned the chase and headed back to Tina.

"You didn't ask about the boy," she hedged. "You'll never catch him back there. He's like a wild thing and knows every tree, gap, and palm frond."

"That sounds like you've said it before. To his father? CPS? Anyone else ever chase him?" Dan was definitely angry.

"And, on top of that, it suddenly just occurred to you where Carl went," he paused for effect.

Tina shrank without even moving. "It might have occurred to me sooner to look for him there." She offered conciliatorily, "Do you need the address?"

"No, actually I don't, thank you." Dan's normal courtesy and affable demeanor deserted him as he marched back to his vehicle.

Dan surveyed the home he had

already searched once. Carl had definitely come here.

There were signs they both had, or maybe Carl had just cleaned out the second bedroom hoping to draw his son in.

Where Carl was *NOW* was a good question...

CHAPTER 23 THURSDAY

Bernie just shook his head. He enjoyed this group of Ralph's, but they were both good-naturedly presumptuous and irritatingly, well, irritatingly presumptuous.

Patty and Catherine had made dinner, meatloaf, potato salad, and corn on the cob. They were laying it out on *HIS* table with *HIS* silverware.

Ralph had told him much earlier not to worry about dinner and had just answered his questions with a wink.

Ralph had gotten there at O-dark-thirty to get started at the butt-crack of dawn on the tree. He'd interrupted a *very* nice dream.

Never growl at volunteer labor.

Quarterback had barked joyfully at Ralph and danced around the chainsaws and the bobcat until Bernie had to yell at him and finally put him in the house with Patches.

"Quarterback? If you name him 'Tight end' I'm taking him back." Ralph just shook his head when Bernie had shut the screen door in front of his rambunctious pup.

"We don't think Doo… Quarterback…

is much of a watchdog. A good dog, but not exactly intimidating," Catherine began.

"Who died and made you the spokesperson?" Ralph asked.

"This is the last night the car is going to be in your barn. If you're smart, you'll sell it while it's at the mechanic's shop." Patty continued.

"That will mean you wasted all that time, effort, and electronic equipment because everyone in town will know where the car is and won't bother coming back out here." Ralph finished.

"So, we're prepared to sacrifice a night's sleep to sit up with you and Doo..., excuse me, Quarterback, here. We'll turn out all the lights and sit with the car."

"I can't see the detective being happy with that."

"He said absolutely not," Dr. Catherine repeated happily.

"How did he know?"

"Someone may have leaked to Myrna at the car club that the car was going to be moved tomorrow and this was the last time it wouldn't be in a lit shop with glass doors in the middle of town," Patty supplied cheerfully.

"And now, of course, the entire town knows."

"Well, maybe not everyone, but seventeen people have called to ask me about it," Ralph contributed.

Bernie took a deep breath and glared at him.

"Well, maybe not seventeen."

"But Dan heard. He called me," added Patty. "I told him we were playing cards tonight. He didn't think to ask where."

"Or else he knew..." said Bernie, darkly.

Carl had convinced the shop to let

him drive a loaner until Caroleen's car was released to him.

Michael shook his head as Carl pulled into Tina's driveway in the peeling black import. *What kind of hold did his dad have over the owner of that shop? He couldn't be that good of a mechanic.*

"You can't have him. The boy needs to finish school. He can stay here."

Carl looked down at his niece. He could squash her like a bug, but she was dictating terms to him.

He liked that in a woman.

She wasn't a woman; she was his niece.

"Michael! Get your butt down here before I flatten your cousin."

Michael appeared on the staircase. "Leave her alone. She's right. I don't have long to go. Then I can get a job and live with you again if you still want me." Independence was important, he loved his cousin and didn't trust his dad.

He would deal with it after graduation when it happened.

"Get your butt out here. I want to talk to you."

"Alone," he growled at Tina.

"What?" Michael snapped and Carl raised his hand to smack the insolence off the boy's face.

Defiance flared in the boy's eyes, so disconcertingly on level with Carl's, but the color of his much shorter mother.

"I heard that fancy car is being moved to town to that shop that specializes in classic and show cars."

"And it has finally dawned on you that if the car was Caroleen's, it should be yours now?"

Michael ducked, but Carl's swing was only half-hearted. "I would think that would interest you, as well. College isn't cheap."

"It's a two-man job, and no one else

will help you – at least no one who wouldn't blurt it out to the bar room next Friday night." Michael had already thought about this.

"It will have to be tonight. Take it to Caroleen's and put it in the garage."

"You don't think that will be the first place they look?" Michael was scornful.

Carl was willing to overlook the tone since the boy was apparently in; he was helping plan, anyway.

"Where do you suggest, *here*?"

"There's a shed near the bog. You could probably throw a rock from the barn to the shed, but you couldn't drive that way. If you can get it started, it'll be about three and a half miles. It can stay there for a week or so until we can move it at night to a storage unit somewhere."

"No one goes there?"

"I go there to – do homework – and things."

Big Foot and the Bentley

CHAPTER 24   STILL THURSDAY

Ralph was sitting on the short dresser on one side of the Bentley's room. Bernie was leaning against the doorframe but had a step stool next to him.

Catherine had nearly begged off and asked Ralph to take her home when she was only half-way across the yard.

"I am so sorry, Miss Catherine," Bernie declared as he took one arm and Ralph took the other to practically carry her over the weeds and yard-high grass to get to the barn.

Patty was carrying her walker as Catherine bad-temperedly snapped back "Dr. Catherine, not Miss!" She hated it when she was unable to navigate something on her own.

"What Bernie means to say is that if we hadn't bullied him into this, and bribed him with beer and meatloaf, it wouldn't matter what his yard looked like," Patty cheerfully added.

"You can't strangle me and carry Catherine at the same time. The impulse will pass by the time we get there."

"She thinks she knows me…" grouched Bernie.

"That's because you're just like her," Catherine explained.

"Except she's better looking," butted in Ralph.

"*And* you're more polite," added Catherine.

While Bernie settled Dr. Catherine onto the rolling chair (cleaned off) that had been there for eons, Ralph returned and brought a folding chair for Patty.

Bernie opened his security app and propped his phone on a shelf. "The cameras are motion sensitive and set to ignore small animals. When they turn on, my phone will beep, and the screen will appear. We should be able to talk quietly in the meantime, or even take turns taking naps since I still doubt anyone is stupid enough to try again."

"Only humoring us, Bro?"

"You, yes. I prefer to think I'm entertaining the ladies."

"*I'm* the one who brought drinks!" With a flourish, Ralph revealed a thermos of coffee, a flask of cream, sugar, five bottles of water, and four bottles of beer.

"That's a magic backpack!" Patty laughed, "five bottles of water?"

"Abra-ca-dabra was my first word," bragged Ralph as he opened one bottle and poured it into a small plastic bowl for Quarterback.

"Your first word was "Uh-oh," Bernie contradicted him. "I know, I was there!"

"Patty's first words were probably "I didn't do it." Dr. Catherine laughed.

"Yours were probably "How do you feel about that?"

"Now, children…"

There was laughter all around, some a little more spontaneous than others.

"So, I did bring cards." Patty reached

into her pocket and drew them out. "We have to play at least one hand of something, so I didn't lie to Dan."

Hours later, Ralph was the only one awake when a tiny beep sounded and the phone screen flickered on. It was very dark, but a large figure was approaching the front door of the barn with a crowbar. A second screen flickered to life and both images got smaller.

Another figure approached from the garden side of the barn. Just as the first one tried to insert the crowbar between the doors, a third screen flickered to life and there was a figure at the corner of the barn.

"Hey, Bernie, wake up," hissed Ralph. "Do you have an overlap on two of the cameras? Or are there three people out there?"

Bernie grabbed his phone and dialed 911. There was a limit to his willingness to play vigilante.

"Don't wake the girls."

The two of them slipped out of that room and toward the inside of the front door. The security app had closed when he dialed. The inept thieves had jammed the crowbar between the doors, but only by a scant inch and was trying to force them open.

Bernie was trying to open the security app again when torchlight illuminated his backyard, lighting up the windows into the barn.

His watchdog woke up, as well as the ladies. A booming voice told Carl to put down the crowbar.

Bernie recognized Dan's voice. He should have known the detective wouldn't just let it go. He'd obviously been close.

As the camera feeds flickered to life again, Bernie saw one of the figures fading into the woods. He hastily ducked out one of the stall doors, since the front ones had been locked from the outside. As he stepped out to try to get a better look,

Quarterback flashed past him and took off into the woods as well.

"I can't steal something that's rightfully mine!" Bernie heard Carl bellow.

Whoever was Dan's partner for the night put handcuffs on the angry thief and stuffed him carefully into the back of the cruiser.

"Another one ran into the woods; my dog ran after him. We'll need your torch." Dan almost argued when Bernie fell in behind him. "Ralph, take care of the women," he called to his brother as they left the circle of light.

"I'm switching it off, so he doesn't see us coming."

Bernie prayed that snakes only came out in daylight. *He was going to start wearing real shoes, he really was.*

The sounds of his spaniel bouncing in the underbrush led them deeper and deeper into the woods. "Doo! Come here." Bernie whispered fiercely.

A warm, furry body pressed against his thigh as he crouched in the underbrush. Dan signaled for him to stay down, and he grasped his dog's collar. The large shed loomed ahead of them. It was one of those with a wide, vehicle door on one side and a pedestrian door on the front. They were facing the large door, with one side propped open with a stick.

What little light the sliver of moon gave was unable to penetrate the canopy above them. Only because their eyes had adapted to the dark during the chase were they able to make out the shape of the shed at all.

They heard a voice inside. "Remember, they don't know you killed Caroleen. It was, after all, kind of an accident. She swung first. There's no way they could prove you were even there; I was the only witness.

"They'll come looking for us tomorrow. Just be cool and deny everything. It stinks in here. Why do you smell like wet wool? What are you wearing? Let's get back to Tina's to get the car."

Michael slipped out the door. Dan switched his light into the boy's eyes. When Michael started to fight, he hooked an ankle behind the boy's left knee and put him on the ground.

"Hold this." Dan tossed the light toward Bernie.

As Bernie grabbed it and stood up, letting go of his dog, the light wavered, and he was sure he saw a shape moving away from the far side of the shed. He reflexively moved the light in that direction and got yelled at by the detective handcuffing Michael.

Doo stared off into the woods but stayed leaning against Bernie's leg.

CHAPTER 25 FRIDAY

Tina sat at Bernie's table, with Ralph, Patty, Catherine, and, of course, Bernie.

"Michael swears he wasn't alone in that shed, and he doesn't have any reason to lie to me."

They all knew that Carl had been in the back of the Sheriff's vehicle.

No one was going to make any guesses about the third shadowy figure in the short video or regarding why Michael thought his dad was right behind him.

There was companionable silence.

Bernie got up and offered coffee or water to them all.

"Tell me Doodle's not in doo-doo for running off," Patty begged.

"He's not in trouble."

"What is his name, today?" Tina asked. At Bernie's raised eyebrows she explained, "Ralph's been keeping track of the names and telling me about them."

"As a disinterested party, then, what

do *you* think I should name him?"

Tina laughed. "Oh, I'm interested! I'm also part Irish. Of all the names Ralph has repeated to me," she looked to Ralph, "I've heard them all, right?"

"I'm pretty sure," Ralph assured her, with an apologetic look to Bernie for gossiping.

"Then I like Gruagach, the Irish Big Foot."

Patty laughed outright, Catherine chuckled, and Ralph shrugged.

Bernie looked down into the adoring eyes of his less-than-vicious watchdog.

"Good dog, Gru."

Doodle put his big paw up and pawed at the air.

Please consider leaving me a review on Amazon or on Goodreads. Reviews are our lifeblood as authors!

Find me at:
https://www.amazon.com/author/maryluscholl

ABOUT THE AUTHOR

Mary Lu Scholl kissed the Blarney Stone and has never looked back.
Retired and living in the paradise of West

Central Florida, on the Nature Coast, she writes cozy mysteries for both men and women. She lives with her mom and a cat, around the corner from her daughter. Family is steadily migrating toward the warm climate and she looks forward to having everyone close.

TRAILER PARK TRAVAILS
PATTY DECKER COZY MYSTERIES

Camper Catastrophe (Book 1)

www.amazon.com/dp/B07MHV48PH

Mobile Mayhem (Book 2)

www.amazon.com/dp/B07MWBL8P

Birds, Bees and RVs (Book 3)

www.amazon.com/dp/B07PM8Z35H

Trailer Trauma (Book 4)

www.amazon.com/dp/B07YCSS9GS

Modular Murder (Book 5)

www.amazon.com/dp/B084T817MG

Corpse in the Clubhouse (Book 6)

www.amazon.com/dp/B08NJ6B2WF

Restless Retirement (Book 7)

www.amazon.com/dp/B093FWNRGY

Motorhome Motives (Book 8)

www.amazon.com/dp/B09CP1FF29

Fatal Philandering (Book 9)

www.amazon.com/dp/B0C47HRXQ6

Dirt, Drugs and Disaster (Book 10)

www.amazon.com/dp/B0D2SGL6TB

Eventually, Patty encounters Bernie Murphy.
Bernie lives nearby and that's where Nature Coast Calamities pick up.
With a hint of Irish Folklore,

NATURE COAST CALAMITIES

BERNIE MURPHY COZY MYSTERIES

Lecanto Leprechaun (Book 1)

www.amazon.com/dp/B09ZKNVL49

Big Foot and the Bentley (Book 2)

www.amazon.com/dp/B0B7QHJKM2

InverNessie (Book 3)

www.amazon.com/dp/B0BCHCSX3B

Pu'ka and the Pirates (Book 4)
www.amazon.com/dp/B0CGBMVHHT

Manufactured by Amazon.ca
Bolton, ON